UNLOCKING THE PAST

index
and CD-ROM of
abstracts of articles

to

THE AMATEUR HISTORIAN
(1952-1967)

and

THE LOCAL HISTORIAN
(1968-1999)

volumes 1-29

compiled by Alan G. Crosby

British Association for Local History
www.balh.co.uk

ISBN 1 86077 171 8

1st edition, 2001

BALH General Editor Alan G. Crosby

© **British Association for Local History 2001**

Designed and printed by Salisbury Printing Company Limited
Greencroft Street SALISBURY SP1 1JF

CONTENTS

Editor's Introduction   4

The Amateur Historian and *The Local Historian*:
a bibliographical essay by Lionel Munby   6

Notes on using the abstracts of articles   12

Table of volumes and years   12

Index of Subjects   13

Index of Places   132

Index of People and Families   146

Index of Authors   150

Index of Reviewers   161

Abstracts of articles 1952-1999   CD-ROM in wallet inside back cover

EDITOR'S INTRODUCTION

In 1952 Terrick FitzHugh founded a new journal, *The Amateur Historian*, editing it himself and producing it on a shoestring. He certainly did not envisage that half a century later, transmogrified into *The Local Historian*, it would have become a widely-respected, authoritative and influential publication, attractive and highly professional in appearance and content, and with a cumulative total of many thousands of pages and many hundreds of articles. Today *The Local Historian* is generally regarded as the most important and valuable local history journal in Britain. That it has achieved this place is a tribute to a succession of dedicated and determined editors, until recent years unremunerated for their hard work, who have sought to maintain and develop the standards and reputation of the journal. Its success and status are also a reflection of the policy of those editors in adhering to some cardinal rules which were laid down at the start of the journal's life and still apply today

- that it should not only seek to inform readers of the researches undertaken by others, but also to inspire them to go forth and carry out their own research and analysis using the methods, sources and approaches discussed in the articles
- that it should not sacrifice quality and weight in favour of a predominance of ephemeral or trivial material
- that it should define local history in a very wide and 'broad church' sense, eschewing academic elitism and an excess of esotericism
- and that it should always draw its material from the widest possible range of contributors to reflect the immensely diverse 'catchment' of the subject

Over the ensuing volumes these principles have been carefully maintained. *The Local Historian* is a journal with lasting - indeed, permanent - value, one destined to be taken down from shelves and consulted over the years to come, rather than being read once and discarded. It provides inspiration to readers, encouraging the wider use of sources and the adoption of different approaches to research and analysis, and informing the local history world about new developments and the latest methodologies. It has, throughout its life, publicised the debates in local history about the philosophies and structure of the subject. It includes a highly-regarded section which authoritatively reviews new publications great and small. Its authors are many and varied, from senior academics of international standing, acknowledged experts on their subject, to those amateur (in the best sense of the word) researchers who are the inheritors of an honoured tradition in English local and family history, and whose contribution to the subject should never, in any circumstance, be undervalued or treated with condescension. *The Local Historian* and its predecessor have frequently been at the forefront of new directions for research, and include articles which have been landmarks in the development of the subject. Over the years, therefore, the journal has become a rich treasury of information about local history in all its many aspects, including the history of local history itself.

In 1998 the Council of the British Association for Local History agreed that it would be appropriate to make this great quantity and diversity of material more readily accessible to local historians everywhere, by publishing a full index to the 29 volumes to the end of 1999, and by preparing short abstracts to each article. The present volume, the complete index 1952-1999, and the accompanying CD-ROM of the abstracts for every article published during this period, represent the coming to fruition of that project. The volume also includes a valuable bibliographical essay on the development of the journal, written by Lionel Munby, Terrick FitzHugh's successor as editor.

We hope that this combined index and abstracts will unlock the riches within the journal and that the two components are suitably 'user-friendly'. One of the outstanding features which I observed in compiling the index and abstracts, a task which involved reading every article, is that a remarkable number of the contributions made thirty or forty years ago remain fresh and lively, stimulating and challenging. Of course, much has changed over that time - most obviously, perhaps, the advent of the computer and its spin-offs, which have transformed the practicalities of local history research, analysis and writing - but the value of many of those articles written decades ago does not diminish. It is fascinating to note the early contributions by those who later became nationally-known figures, and to see how tentative conclusions, hesitatingly expressed in the 1960s and 1970s, have now become cornerstones of methodology or interpretation. I hope, therefore, that readers will be encouraged to re-read earlier volumes, or turn to them for the first time, and that in their own particular areas of interest and research they will identify useful material.

This is the first comprehensive index to *The Amateur Historian* and *The Local Historian*, but 'Short Indexes' have been compiled and printed regularly during the life of the journal. In recent years these have been prepared by Diana Munby, and I would like to express our very grateful thanks to her for this work, which the Council of B.A.L.H. and all readers and users of the journal have much appreciated. With regard to the present volume, I would like to give particular thanks to Simon Fitzpatrick, who did valuable preliminary work in the preparation of this index and the accompanying abstracts; to David Dymond, whose very helpful suggestions and careful proof-reading were greatly appreciated; to Lionel Munby, one of the great figures of post-war local history in England, for writing the introductory essay; to Rose Turner, for her invaluable help in proof-reading the abstracts; and to members of the Council of the British Association for Local History not only for supporting this project but also for their very helpful comments on layout, content and style. There may be errors, few I hope. They are mine.

Alan G. Crosby

THE AMATEUR HISTORIAN AND *THE LOCAL HISTORIAN*:

A BIBLIOGRAPHICAL ESSAY
BY LIONEL MUNBY

On two occasions I have been asked to look back on the history of *The Amateur Historian* and *The Local Historian*. To repeat the content of these articles, which were published in August 1977 and February 1992,[1] would be superfluous. Much further information can also be found in past editorials, especially those of Terrick FitzHugh, the founder and first editor of *The Amateur Historian*, and in occasional editorials by later editors which deal with the policy of the journal.[2] Of course, many more editorials comment on developments in the world of local history. There were memorial 'appreciations' of the journal's creative first Reviews Editor, Robin Chaplin, and of Terrick FitzHugh himself.[3] From these features all the major developments in the history of the journal up to the 1990s can be followed.

There were many crises, financial, organisational and of personalities. There have been seven editors, six publishers (or persons effectively responsible for ensuring the journal's appearance) and eleven printers. However, the journal has survived because ordinary people who loved local history have wanted it to, and it has enormously improved in appearance and size without any great increase in real price. Neither wealthy patrons, businesses, nor academic institutions have controlled or directly helped it, though many university teachers, especially from adult education departments, have been contributors and subscribers.

The Local Historian is a unique journal. This alone would make a comprehensive index valuable, but it is in considering the quality, variety and pioneering role of its contents that its importance clearly emerges. My belief is that in five decades a great deal of lasting importance has appeared in its pages. Of course it may be said that as a former editor I am prejudiced. However, I ceased to be editor a quarter of a century ago, and there have been five editors since.[4]

The Local Historian has served its readers in many different ways and it has also developed the understanding and practice of major aspects of British history as a whole. Central to its aims and purposes from the beginning has been the publication of articles suggesting themes to study, sources to explore, and methods of using them. A glance at the footnotes in almost any book about sources for local historians will make clear how many and how varied these have been. Such articles have increasingly been supplemented over time by those which have demonstrated by example, through a particular piece of local history, how to use the sources available for specific topics. These have grown in number in recent years and under Margaret Bonney's editorship grew longer. It has never been an editorial aim as such to publish articles on the local history of the widest possible area, but past issues do contain a wealth of local history from most parts of the country.

Probably all this more than justifies the production of this index, but much more can be found in the journal's files. *The Local Historian* has been a major influence in spreading knowledge and understanding of many of the new developments in historical scholarship since the end of the Second World War. On some important occasions it has in effect pioneered them. The Vernacular Architecture Group and the Deserted Medieval Village

Research Group were formed by small bands of enthusiasts in 1952. In 1953 and 1954 two articles by Margery Roberts appeared in *The Amateur Historian*, with examples of ways in which 'an old house offers material for interesting research'.[5] In 1955 an article on 'Deserted Medieval Villages' by J. G. Hurst, then Secretary of the DMVRG, made the point that 'in this study the help of local amateurs is necessary and welcome'.[6] This was not the last occasion on which this kind of comment was made. Kenneth Hudson, in his pioneering *Industrial Archaeology* (1963) pointed out that the term's first appearance in print was in the autumn of 1955, in an article written by Michael Rix for *The Amateur Historian*. I commissioned that article, on 'the archaeology of the industrial revolution', and Michael Rix replied that he would be delighted to do one on *Industrial Archaeology*.[7] The title became internationally-accepted, introduced to German scholars, for example, in 1975 when it was suggested that 'Industrial Archaeology had developed in Great Britain as a scholarly research subject with an inter-disciplinary character'. The name and activity 'came out of local history and adult education circles in England' and the *Amateur Historian* article was noted.[8]

In 1964 I met Tony Wrigley when he was working on his experimental family reconstitution for Colyton in Devon. I asked him to explain the method and to suggest how amateur local historians could help with the major national project just being launched by the newly-formed Cambridge Group for the History of Population and Social Structure. His two articles in 1964 and 1965 played a part in creating the teams which supported the Cambridge Group.[9] A new popular specialism among local historians came into existence which in 1968 produced its own journal, *Local Population Studies*, and in 1973 its own society.

In an article in June 1976, 'New horizons in local history', Alan Rogers analysed the explosion of new journals and new societies for new historical specialisms which took place in the two decades from the early 1950s.[10] In 1950 the would-be local historian, whether practitioner or teacher, could consult a wealth of traditional county histories and similar histories of particular localities, but guidance on sources, demography, landscape history or the history of vernacular buildings, for example, was not available. By the middle of the 1970s it was already beginning to be the case that one hardly had time to read all the specialist literature with which one should be familiar, never mind the many examples of up-to-date local histories, or to decide which 'how to do it' book to recommend to students.

Until the 1970s the journal had kept up reasonably well with all new developments its files reflect the changes and provide a convenient overview. From the late 1970s the task of the editor was changing. An enormous variety of interesting articles on apparently marginal topics were published. A few random examples will give the flavour: bus services; holiday resorts; house repopulation; and churchyard memorials.[11] Robin Chaplin commented in a review article in November 1980 that 'if local history has at this moment one defining characteristics, it is that the subject is exploding outwards from its solid core of parish history, casting particles in all directions'. Kate Tiller took up this theme in an editorial of August 1983. Local history had changed since *The Amateur Historian* first appeared in August 1952 and 'we need to try to catch the particles sometimes, and attempt to make sense of them'. This is what editors did. Articles on the themes just mentioned sought to show how their study could be integrated into, and so enlarge, the scope of local histories.[12]

Concern with new approaches continued. In November 1989 there were articles on computerisation and the value of photographs.[13] The latter, which described Victorian photography, was related to the publication of pictorial evidence which David Dymond had introduced in February 1980 with a series of 'Historical Photographs'. This was no doubt inspired in part by Norman McCord's 'Photographs as historical evidence' which had been published two years before.[14] The series continued until November 1985, when it was succeeded by 'Historical Illustrations', including maps, engravings and documents. When this series ended in November 1987 a series of articles on local photographers and their work carried on the theme until November 1990.

Guidance through the forest, attempting to make sense of the expanding jungle of specialisms, was provided by a series of articles under the headings 'Sources for ... ' between 1970 and 1976.[15] The topics covered included agricultural history, church history, Scottish history and urban history, each with four or more articles. In November 1983 Kate Tiller announced a series entitled 'What to read on ... ': 'the idea is to get historians working on major themes or periods to introduce some of the best, most useful and accessible books amongst the mass being produced'.[16] They covered a great diversity of topics, including religious history, children, the history of Wales, place-names and military history. The series continued until August 1987.

The Amateur Historian and *The Local Historian* have not only covered an extremely wide range of subjects but the editors have also encouraged a galaxy of talent by publishing the early work of many historians who later became nationally and internationally known. In the first two and a half years of its existence the proprietor, Terrick FitzHugh, published articles by a remarkable group of young archivists and local historians as well as by established academics. Later editors did their best to maintain that golden standard. Some of the contributors were listed in my 1992 article. In the first fifteen years of the journal's existence they included Alan Everitt, G.E. Fussell, W.G. Hoskins and Joan Thirsk. Margaret Gelling wrote an article on place-names in the second issue of *The Amateur Historian* and has contributed frequently thereafter, her most recent article being in August 1992 on 'The present state of English place-name studies'.[17] John Marshall has been an equally regular contributor since his combative article in the autumn of 1963, on which more later.[18] Many articles on related topics followed, the latest, in February 1996, on the problem of defining the local community.[19] A leading amateur local historian from Hertfordshire, William Branch Johnson, wrote seven articles between 1953 and 1966. Over the twelve years in which David Dymond and Kate Tiller were editors, 1976 to 1988, new contributors of the same quality appeared: F.G. Emmison, Pamela Horn and Christopher Taylor, for example, and more recently authors have included nationally-known figures such as John Walton and Richard Muir.

The two most recent editors, Philip Morgan and Margaret Bonney, have continued the tradition of *The Local Historian*, maintaining the great variety and high quality of articles published. In her first editorial Margaret Bonney renewed the pledge which Terrick FitzHugh had given in 1952 that the journal was to be devoted to historical enquiry as a popular activity. This was not to be another periodical catering for the professional or the specialist historian.[20] A rough analysis of the contributions edited by Philip Morgan and Margaret Bonney from 1988 reveals how the original philosophy of the journal has been faithfully maintained. Almost half of the authors were unconnected with the world of academic history, and they included civil servants, a solicitor, a prison governor, a mariner-pilot, and a taxi driver. Of course many people could have been put in two or more categories, and many of the non-professional contributors had had all kinds of training in the study of local history, but the 'broad church' of the local history world is quite clearly well represented.

It was such people who wrote on some less usual topics. One contributor, who at the time worked in the computing department of the Central Electricity Generating Board, wrote a statistical article on the diffusion of English surnames. A botanist produced a population study of nurse-children. The prison governor wrote of the development of coal-mining on

Yorkshire landed estates. A retired physiotherapist wrote about eighteenth century chain surveyors, while a retired professor of civil and public health engineering described the British Book Trade Index. A retired civil servant who had begun his working life as a baker wrote about the Loughton Mutual Labor-Aid Society 1891-1899. An economics lecturer wrote of changes in the public house in north-east England between the wars, and another lecturer discussed cricket and Christianity in Lancashire 1900-1939. None of these articles is amateurish in the derogatory sense. Instead, they are fully up to the standards of those in other academic journals while remaining accessible and informative to a non-academic readership. They illustrate the immense wealth of history which this new index reveals to all.[21]

Writing local history involves much more than compiling a narrative history of a particular locality. What local history is, and how it has changed over time, has been a matter for continuous debate throughout the life of the journal. Local history, at least as understood today, is a new discipline - if it is a discipline at all - and its practitioners have, not surprisingly, taken some time to decide what it is and have still not reached a clear conclusion. In the autumn of 1963 John Marshall challenged readers of *The Amateur Historian* to think about it. Should the local historian attempt to research and write the history of a local geographical area, or only study limited themes locally. Dr Marshall attacked the Leicester School for their 'emphasis on a geographical boundary, that of the parish', and for a parallel stress on training local historians in records and 'how to do it' 'Even the veriest beginner [should] be presented with a problem [and] the historian's tools, ideas'. Parish history could become an arid accumulation of facts without real historical discovery. For this a wider area, the region, in which comparisons could be made, was important.[22]

A major discussion, a debate, continued throughout volume 6 (1964-1965) and intermittently in later years. Alan Everitt and Donald Read clarified the 'geographical boundary' argument. Everitt's view was that 'a local community must have some kind of boundary or it is not local'. It should have 'a definite sense of its organic unity'. For most people before the nineteenth century this was the town or village. Only 'the gentry, and perhaps the yeomanry [had the] wider sense of a county or regional locality'. As for the themes which Marshall proposed, they were not necessarily local history: 'the biography of an outstanding personality', for example, was simple biography. Donald Read pointed out that taking 'the small local area as the unit for study' after the industrial revolution led to concentration on 'the decline of the local community', which was hardly relevant to the history of Birmingham or Manchester. 'In modern local history the inter-relation between the local and the national must be established. A parochial approach must be discarded. It may be significant that the first uses known to the OED of "parochial" in the sense of "narrowness of view" come from the middle of the nineteenth century, when the railways had just made their great impact'.[23]

In February 1989 Kevin Schurer suggested that 'the relationship and interactions between one type of spatial unit and its neighbours' should not be seen, as Finberg had seen it, simply as 'a series of concentric circles: family, local community, national state'.[24] What mattered was 'when studying a local community to understand how it relates to the constellation of communities which surround it and of which it is a part'. 'The position of the antiquary' was defended by David Cox in the summer of 1965 and later by Victor Skipp, who pointed out that the 'total reconstitution' which was fashionable by the 1980s needed the text of every single document.[25] This the antiquarian aimed at while 'narrative and analytical historians select facts and *discard* facts'. Skipp made this comment in May and August 1981 in his most satisfying and all-embracing 'New definition of local history'. He quoted Finberg's study of Withington and Wrigley's work on Colyton to show that a parish could be used for 'formulating concepts and establishing generalisations' just as well as a region. In 1965 Skipp had quoted his own 'discovery' classes in five parishes on the outskirts of Birmingham to argue that parish and regional history could be complementary. These classes produced material which could be, and in 1978 was, used for a regional study, *Crisis and development an ecological case study of the Forest of Arden 1570-1674*.

In so many different ways the past numbers of *The Amateur Historian* and *The Local Historian* are rich in ideas and information which a good index and set of abstracts will at last make easily available to the local historian who comes to the study fresh but wanting to know, and to the experienced historian who is developing new research. This book is a most welcome addition to the historian's armoury.

Lionel Munby

1. *TLH* 12 07 330-337 and 22 01 8-13
2. e.g. *TLH* 14 06; 15 07; 16 03; 18 03; 20 03; 22 01; and 27 01
3. *TLH* 18 02 and 22 01
4. See table below
5. *TAH* 01 08 and 01 12
6. *TAH* 02 07
7. *TAH* 02 08
8. Akos Paulinyi, *Industriearchaologie: Neue Aspekte der Wirtschafts-und-Technikgeschichte* (1975) Gesellschaft für Westfälische Wirtschaftsgeschichte, eV Dortmund, Ostwall 51
9. *TAH* 06 05 and 06 06
10. *TLH* 12 02
11. *TLH* 13 05; 15 04; 13 06; 13 02; 14 03; and 13 03
12. *TLH* 14 04 and 15 07
13. *TLH* 15 08
14. *TLH* 14 01
15. *TLH* 09 02 and 12 01
16. *TLH* 15 08. They ran from 16 01 to 17 07.
17. *TLH* 22 03
18. *TAH* 06 01
19. *TLH* 26 01
20. *TLH* 22 01
21. *TLH* 19 02; 19 03; 23 04; 24 02; 24 04; 25 01 and 25 02
22. *TAH* 06 01
23. *TAH* 06 02 and 06 04
24. *TLH* 19 01
25. *TAH* 06 08; *TLH* 14 06 and 14 07

Editors of *The Amateur Historian* and *The Local Historian*

Terrick FitzHugh	Summer 1952 to Winter 1954-1955
Lionel Munby	Spring 1955 to November 1975
David Dymond	February 1976 to November 1982
Kate Tiller	February 1983 to February 1988
Philip Morgan	August 1988 to November 1991
Margaret Bonney	February 1992 to August 2001
Alan Crosby	November 2001 onwards

Publishers and printers of *The Amateur Historian* and *The Local Historian*

01	01	H.P. Jolowicz	Sussex Printers (Eastbourne)
		C.E. Fisher & Co. Ltd	
03	01		Foundry Press (Bedford)
03	05	John Cutworth	Kenion Press (Slough)
		Alden and Blackwell	
		Eton College	
04	06		Harwood Press (Harrow)
05	01	National Council of	Blackfriars Press
		Social Service	(Leicester)
12	05		Alfred Peacock (Stanton)
14	01		Charles Clarke (Haywards Heath)
14	02	National Council for	
		Voluntary Organisations	
16	02	BALH (Bedford Square)	
16	03	BALH (Cromford)	
16	06		Ziprint Parchment (Oxford)
17	08	BALH and Phillimore	
18	04		George Street Press (Stafford)
19	04		Titus Wilson (Kendal)
20	01		George Street Press (Stafford)
25	01	BALH (Salisbury)	Salisbury Printing Co.

The price of *The Amateur Historian* and *The Local Historian*

01	01	9s [45p] per annum	0.23p per page
03	01	12s [60p]	0.34p
04	01	18s [90p]	0.50p
05	01	14s [70p]	0.51p
08	01	14s [70p]	0.45p
09	01	£1.05	0.49p
11	01	£1.50	0.60p
13	01	£2.50	0.98p
14	01	£3.00	1.17p
15	02	£5.00	1.95p
17	01	£6.00	2.34p
18	02	£6.00	3.10p
20	01	£7.00	3.50p
22	01	£15.00	6.19p
23	01	£19.00	7.91p
24	01	£19.00	7.42p
29	01	£19.00	6.98p

NB These figures do not take account of inflation or of the other publications such as Newsletters and *Local History News* which over the years have been included with *The Local Historian*.

NOTES ON USING THE ABSTRACTS OF ARTICLES

The text on the CD-ROM comprises a short abstract of every article which appeared in *The Amateur Historian* and *The Local Historian* between 1952 and 1999 (volumes 1-29). The abstracts are arranged in chronological order, so that the first section of each entry gives the bibliographical details. These details cross-reference with the index entries. The example below will illustrate this

09 02 82-88
Chaplin, Robin   Discovering lost ironworks and other industrial remains of the early modern period

Here the article is in volume 9, issue no.2, pages 82-88; the author is Robin Chaplin; and the full title of the article is 'Discovering lost ironworks and other industrial remains of the early modern period'. A typical index entry for this article would be

industries   iron   09   02   82-88

The abstracts have been designed to include all the important points which the article covers, but it should be noted that more recent articles (and especially those since the mid-1980s) tend to have longer entries than those in earlier volumes. This is partly because the later articles are almost always substantially longer, but it also reflects the fact that these articles are more likely to be topical and to contain contemporary or near-contemporary views, methodologies and themes. Conversely, it is essential to note that most earlier articles which refer to the location of source material, its accessibility or its arrangement will be out of date in these details. The date of each article is not given separately, but the covering year or years of each volume are given in the table below.

Articles are cross-referenced (usually at the end of the abstract) either if they are parts of a longer article by the same author which has been subdivided, or if they are in response to another article, or if they in turn generated an article in response. The index is designed to provide the necessary cross-referencing information. Note particularly that the index has listings of bibliographies and glossaries.

The main categories of material which have not been included in the abstracts are i) letters and pages of readers' views and comment (unless the item is of unusual length and depth); ii) news items, current information and short notes on contemporary events; iii) reviews, notices of publications and details of publishing projects; and iv) editorial sections unless these are in the form of an extended comment which amounts to a small article.

Table of volumes and years

volume 1	1952-1955	volume 9	1970-1971	volume 17	1986-1987	volume 25	1995
volume 2	1955-1957	volume 10	1972-1973	volume 18	1988	volume 26	1996
volume 3	1958-1959	volume 11	1974-1975	volume 19	1989	volume 27	1997
volume 4	1960-1961	volume 12	1976-1977	volume 20	1990	volume 28	1998
volume 5	1962-1963	volume 13	1978-1979	volume 21	1991	volume 29	1999
volume 6	1964-1965	volume 14	1980-1981	volume 22	1992		
volume 7	1966-1967	volume 15	1982-1983	volume 23	1993		
volume 8	1968-1969	volume 16	1984-1985	volume 24	1994		

INDEX OF SUBJECTS

During the 47 years to the end of 1999, and 29 volumes of *The Amateur Historian* and *The Local Historian* many thousands of subjects were covered in greater or lesser depth. The complexity and scale of such a large amount of material mean that 'total indexing', in which every passing or incidental reference would be included, has not been practical. Therefore, the entries given below refer to those subjects which have been central to individual articles or where significant detail has been provided in a case-study within an article. In this way all important occurrences of subjects and topics have been indexed but casual references have not.

The nature of local history, and indeed of history in general, means that many users will be looking for all entries on particular broad themes: thus, while some researchers will be specifically investigating, for example, apprentices in the cutlery trade, most of those who would find articles on this subject of interest or relevance will be initially looking at more general themes, such as apprenticeships, industrial history, or labour history. It has therefore seemed most appropriate to make extensive use of general thematic headings which relate to broad categories of information, as well as to disperse specialised entries through the index in alphabetical order. The index is therefore arranged both to include the specific entries (e.g. cutlery trade) but also to place these entries under a variety of more general categories (e.g. apprentices, industries, etc.). We have also sought to cross-reference entries so that users can identify other possible headings which may be of interest.

The following is a list of the more important of the general headings. It is recommended that any user of the index should first refer to this list to ascertain whether the material is likely to have been indexed in one or more of these broad categories. Note that because most articles refer wholly or in part to 'sources' or 'documents', neither of these is given as a general heading - they would have been disproportionately large - but a category entitled 'archive sources' refers to such material in the context of archival holdings. The category headed 'research techniques' includes any articles which relate primarily to theory or methodology, but articles on the practical application of techniques in case-study form will usually be found under the relevant subject headings.

GENERAL THEMATIC HEADINGS

accounts
agricultural history
agricultural labourers
agriculture
apprentices
archaeology
architecture
archive services
archive sources
archives (general)
bibliographies
biography
boundaries
buildings
business history
cartography
census data
census returns
censuses
charity and philanthropy
charters
children
churches
Civil War
clergy
coal-mining
commerce and trade
community history
computing
conservation
counties
courts
crime and punishment
customs and traditions
dating methods
diaries
directories, trade
disease and illness
education (current)
education history

enclosure
estate management
ethnic history
family and kinship
farms
fields
finance and accounting
food and drink
gardens and parks
genealogy and family history
glossaries
health and medical care
heritage
historians and antiquarians
housing
industrial history
industries
inns and public houses
labour history
land ownership
land tenure
landscape history
language
law and order
legal system
leisure and entertainment
libraries
literacy
literature
local government
local history
manorial history
maps and plans
maritime history
markets
memorials and monuments
migration

military history
museums
music
newspapers
nonconformity
occupations and employment
oral history
Ordnance Survey
parish and township administration
parish registers
photographs
place-names
politics, local
Poor Law
population and demography
population mobility
prices
probate records
public health
sculpture and carving
seaside resorts
social history
societies and organisations
sport and recreation
surnames
taxation and rates
tenancy
tourism
towns
trade unions
trades and crafts
transport
urban history
villages
war
women

INDEX OF SUBJECTS

subject	sub-heading	vol	no	pages
accounts	see also *finance and accounting; taxation and rates*			
	borough chamberlains'	02	10	293-296
	business	21	02	76-78
	chapel	15	01	41-43
	charities	27	03	144-162
	churchwardens	01	08	234-237
	collieries 18th c	14	03	156-163
	constables'	01	11	335-338
	estate	11	07	406-413
		25	04	231-241
	evidence for 'country'	26	01	36-47
	farm notebooks	13	05	270-276
	Fell, Sarah	26	01	36-47
	friendly societies	24	04	229-242
	highway surveyors	01	10	301-304
	household	16	08	467-477
	manorial	01	04	112-117
	Merton College Oxford	28	01	16-23
	militia	01	11	335-338
	miscellaneous	01	12	374-377
	monastic	04	04	134-139
	municipal	02	10	293-296
	overseers'	01	09	269-272
		14	01	11-17
		16	01	15-20
		20	01	9-19
	parochial	20	01	9-19
	parson's	13	07	397-405
	probate	21	02	51-59
	tithe	14	01	24-27
Admiralty, The		02	07	207-211
		08	05	160-166
	marine charts	08	03	86-97
adult education	see also *education (current); local history*			
	group projects	24	01	28-35
	local history	10	08	385-389
	local history classes	22	02	58-67
advertisements	farm sales	09	07	334-337
		28	01	36-49
	newspapers	09	07	334-337
		10	06	271-276
	retailing	29	03	167-182
	traders 18th c	17	06	343-350
	urban history	14	03	134-141
agricultural history	see also *agriculture; estate management; farms; landscape history; maps and plans; rural settlement; tithes*			
	agricultural returns	04	02	49-55
	agricultural revolution	09	07	323-333
	animal feeds	23	02	85-91
	animal medicine	03	06	237-248
	apprentices	12	03-04	139-145
	auction catalogues	13	03	131-139

subject	sub-heading	vol	no	pages
agricultural history *(cont.)*	barns	27	02	66-77
	bibliography	09	07	323-333
	boundary charters	27	01	18-29
	Cardiganshire [Ceredigion]	09	04	178-183
	census evidence	27	03	130-143
	college estates	28	01	16-23
	commissary court records	17	01	4-10
	computer databases	26	02	89-101
	Cornwall 1500-1910	04	08	338-345
	counting systems	14	05	282-283
		15	01	21-23
	county councils	23	01	31-39
	development 1500-1900	09	07	323-333
	developments in	15	03	157-160
	Domesday 1910	16	05	282-283
	ecclesiastical records	05	02	44-50
	Elizabethan field books	15	02	67-69
	estate accounts	11	07	406-413
	estate maps	05	03	66-71
	equity court records	17	07	408-416
	farm accounts	11	07	406-413
	farm buildings	12	08	407-420
	farm households	27	03	130-143
	farm inventories	12	05	228-234
	farm notebooks	13	05	270-276
	farm records	12	08	407-420
	farm sales	09	07	334-337
		28	01	36-49
	farm servants	02	11	334-336
	farm sizes	12	02	88-92
		14	05	262-269
		26	01	16-35
		27	03	130-143
	farmers, wealth of	04	05	186-195
	farming communities	09	04	178-183
	feet of fines	24	02	66-82
	field-names	02	12	353-356
		13	07	388-396
		14	05	262-269
		17	05	285-289
	field patterns	04	02	73-77
		05	01	23-28
		05	03	66-71
		14	05	262-269
	final concords	14	07	411-416
	forest law	03	07	305-307
	French peasant risings	11	04	188-199
	glossaries	04	04	152-153
		04	05	195-197
		04	07	291-295
	historiography	09	07	323-333
	horseshoes	03	03	102-104

INDEX OF SUBJECTS

subject	sub-heading	vol	no	pages
agricultural history *(cont.)*	hundred rolls	05	01	9-16
	husbandry books	13	04	195-204
	indexes	19	01	18-20
	inheritance patterns	26	01	16-35
	inventories	04	05	186-195
	labour costs	11	07	406-413
	labour relations	03	02	49-54
		11	03	134-141
	labourer's diary	12	03-04	139-145
	labourers' cottages	10	07	327-334
	land holdings	18	01	16-18
		27	03	130-143
	land market	12	07	337-341
		26	01	16-35
	land tax	06	05	152-156
		15	03	161-165
	land use, medieval	24	02	66-82
	land use patterns	04	02	49-55
		04	08	338-345
		17	04	205-211
	land-use, pre-Conquest	27	01	18-29
	land valuation	16	05	282-283
	landowners 19th c	11	03	134-141
	late Victorian decline	15	08	474-477
	living standards	03	02	49-54
	manorial system	01	03	82-85
	maps and plans	03	03	115-120
	market development	29	04	194-211
	mechanisation	09	04	178-183
		09	07	323-333
	memoranda rolls	05	08	242-246
	mills	02	06	172-175
		07	06	192-195
	mining pollution	24	03	130-138
	moated sites	05	02	34-38
	model communities	16	01	4-14
	model farms	12	08	407-420
	newspaper advertisements	09	07	334-337
		10	06	271-276
		28	01	36-49
	Norfolk	04	01	1-7
	Northumberland	12	03-04	139-145
	Norwegian	15	03	147-154
	occupations employment	09	04	178-183
	oral history	09	07	338-343
	parish records in	06	04	110-114
	parson's accounts	13	07	397-405
	peasant communities	11	04	188-206
	place names	26	02	66-79
	prices	11	07	406-413
	probate accounts	21	02	51-59
	probate inventories	12	05	228-234

subject	sub-heading	vol	no	pages
agricultural history *(cont.)*	probate inventories *(cont.)*	16	03	133-145
		16	04	217-227
		17	02	85-100
	property deeds	10	01	7-12
	recent developments	12	01	18-25
	reinterpretations 1955-80	14	04	195-201
	relict hedgerows	18	02	65-68
	ridge and furrow	05	01	23-28
		07	03	95-98
	Rothamsted research station	23	02	85-91
	rural housing	16	06	323-326
	rural social structure	28	04	194-207
	school attendance	15	08	474-477
	Scottish sources	01	12	374-377
		17	01	4-10
	seasonal employment	09	04	178-183
	smallholdings	11	04	200-206
		17	01	31-38
	sociology of villages	06	08	271-278
	sources (general)	07	01	7-13
	surveying in 18th c	23	04	218-226
	terminology	01	03	86-89
	terriers	01	12	361-364
	tithe records	12	02	88-92
		14	01	24-27
		14	05	262-269
		17	04	205-211
	trade unions	11	03	134-141
		13	05	259-262
		13	06	353-359
	upland estates	26	02	66-79
	urban markets in 17th c	20	03	128-136
	village morphology	09	05	233-241
	Wales	07	05	154-160
	wartime experience	29	02	76-90
	weights and measures	06	04	115-117
	yeoman farmers	26	01	16-35
		28	04	194-207
Agricultural History, Institute of		19	01	18-20
Agricultural History Review		04	04	154-156
agricultural labourers		03	02	49-54
		09	07	338-343
		15	01	25-32
		16	01	15-20
		26	01	16-35
		27	03	130-143
		29	02	66-75
		29	02	76-90
	apprentices	12	03-04	139-145
	oral history	10	07	334-339
	migration	14	01	35-43
	unionism among	13	06	353-359

INDEX OF SUBJECTS

subject	sub-heading	vol	no	pages
agricultural labourers	women	27	03	130-143
agricultural returns		04	02	49-55
agriculture	see also *agricultural history; enclosure; estate management; landscape history; rural settlement*			
	allotments	11	03	134-141
	arable farming	04	01	1-7
		04	05	186-195
		04	08	338-345
	arable Durham 19th c	17	04	205-211
	bee-keeping	29	03	130-151
	cheese-making	13	05	270-276
	common land	07	07	232-240
	crop experimentation	23	02	85-91
	crops, introduction of	04	01	1-7
	crops, inventory evidence	16	04	217-227
		17	02	85-100
	Domesday evidence	01	09	261-264
		01	10	297-300
		01	11	344-347
	dunes, planting on	28	04	242-244
	Dutch influences	04	01	1-7
	enclosure	01	06	178-181
		07	08	265-274
		05	07	218-220
		12	01	18-25
		12	07	337-341
		25	02	77-87
		25	03	164-177
	enclosure disputes	15	07	388-401
	enclosure laws	14	06	352-357
	enclosure, upland	26	02	66-79
	encroachments on waste	11	03	141-147
	farms 19th century	03	07	292-298
	forest management	26	02	66-79
	forests, medieval	28	04	194-207
	game protection	26	03	142-154
	hedgerows	13	04	195-204
	improvements	04	08	338-345
	livestock advertisements	28	01	36-49
	livestock 19th c	12	03-04	139-145
		13	05	270-276
	livestock Durham 19th c	17	04	205-211
	livestock farming	04	05	186-195
		04	08	338-345
		16	04	217-227
		17	02	85-100
		17	05	285-289
	livestock in inventories	12	05	228-234
	open fields	04	02	73-77
		05	01	23-28
	parks	03	08	332-349
	rabbits	09	02	59-64

subject	sub-heading	vol	no	pages
agriculture *(cont.)*	rabbits *(cont.)*	18	01	13-15
		18	02	53-57
	sheep farming	04	04	134-139
	upland enclosure	26	02	66-79
	wartime controls	29	02	76-90
	woodland	16	02	73-82
		20	02	73-79
	woodland management	27	02	66-77
Allan Ramsay Library		19	02	58-62
allotments		11	03	134-141
almanacs		03	02	66-69
Amateur Historian		22	01	8-13
Anglo-Saxon studies		25	01	3-6
antiquarians		03	01	20-31
	Cheshire 19th c	26	01	3-14
	Welsh	11	01	7-13
anti-Semitism	Glasgow in 1930s	27	02	106-117
apprentices	agricultural	12	03-04	139-145
	cutlery trade	25	04	194-208
	deposition evidence	17	05	269-276
	freemen's rolls	09	02	89-95
	initiation rites	11	02	72-76
	migration	08	07	232-236
	New Poor Law and	19	02	51-55
	paupers	14	07	400-406
	records	02	12	357-361
		08	07	232-236
		14	01	11-17
	social/family status	25	04	194-208
	terms of	25	04	194-208
Arabs	merchant seamen in North East	27	04	225-244
archaeology	aerial photographs	15	07	402-405
	anecdotes concerning	01	05	134-139
	Anglo-Saxon	25	01	3-6
	bee-keeping	29	03	130-151
	coins	02	01	1-3
	Dark Ages	02	03	72-75
	deserted villages	02	07	193-196
		13	08	471-474
	early carved stones	04	04	140-142
	early factory sites	09	04	183-189
	fieldwork	03	01	1-8
		05	04	115-120
	general	01	05	134-139
		01	06	187-190
		02	05	141-144
		03	04	170-174
	industrial	02	08	225-229
		05	02	56-60
		09	02	82-88
		12	06	296-303
	Ironbridge Museums	09	06	289-293

subject	sub-heading	vol	no	pages
archaeology *(cont.)*	Kings Lynn survey	08	04	139-145
	landscape history and	16	08	483-488
	Ordnance Survey	05	06	166-172
	pottery	01	12	378-381
		02	06	161-164
	rabbits, evidence for	18	02	53-57
	rescue	08	04	139-145
	resistivity testing	03	04	153-159
	Roman inscriptions	02	10	289-292
	scientific approaches	03	04	153-159
architecture	see also *buildings; churches; housing; and names of individual building types/categories*			
	barns	27	02	66-77
	baths, public	25	03	142-152
	beerhouses	17	08	457-464
	bibliography	07	03	92-94
		17	02	78-84
	Bristol, medieval	28	01	3-15
	building plans	17	08	457-464
		19	01	3-7
		19	03	120-123
	building styles	18	04	183-186
	cemeteries 19th c	28	03	130-144
	changing fashions in	14	02	68-75
		18	04	183-186
	chapels	21	01	4-10
	chimneys	01	08	252-255
	church monuments	02	12	362-365
	church restoration	21	03	120-125
	church towers	08	08	282-287
	church wafer ovens	07	05	161-165
	churches	05	04	107-10
		07	01	17-27
		07	02	53-59
	cinemas	20	03	118-122
	cities 19th c	09	08	400-406
	cottages	01	12	365-367
		10	07	327-332
		16	01	4-14
	documentary evidence	12	05	235-240
	domestic	07	04	126-132
	ecclesiastical 19th c	27	02	91-105
	estate villages	28	04	208-216
	farm buildings	12	08	407-420
	fire insurance plans	11	06	343-349
	fonts	23	03	130-145
	garden villages	27	01	30-47
	Georgian buildings	14	02	68-75
	glebe terrier evidence	08	02	47-53
	Gothic traditions	02	07	197-201
	graffiti drawings	23	01	4-19
	house recording	15	01	6-20

subject	sub-heading	vol	no	pages
architecture *(cont.)*	housing 1930s	28	02	94-107
	housing (inventories)	04	04	157-161
	hunting lodges	26	02	66-79
	inventory evidence	02	03	76-79
	inventory Kip engravings	04	01	23-25
	market halls	08	04	118-125
	model farms	12	08	407-420
	monasteries	01	06	187-191
	mosques	28	04	225-241
	Pevsner, Nikolaus	15	08	454-455
	pleasure gardens	03	08	319-324
	priest-holes	06	08	266-269
	public houses	25	01	31-42
	re-fronting	18	04	183-186
	Sherborne Castle	25	04	231-241
	stonemasons	21	02	60-65
	subterranean passages	02	02	33-36
	terminology (churches)	02	01	15-18
	textile mills 18th c	15	05	277-287
	timber-framing	27	02	66-77
	timber supplies	27	02	66-77
	town houses	14	02	68-75
	vernacular buildings	12	02	81-84
		12	05	235-240
		16	06	323-326
		17	02	78-84
	VCH coverage	22	03	128-137
	visual images	09	08	400-406
	Whitby 19th c	28	02	78-93
archive services	see also *archives (general); libraries*			
	accommodation	22	02	74-83
	Bedfordshire	21	01	11-15
	British Records Association	03	07	283-285
	Caernarvonshire Record Office	08	01	22-27
	Chetham's Library	20	01	31-6
	Czechoslovakia	05	08	247-250
	Danish	05	07	221-224
	development of	06	02	45-48
		22	02	74-83
	English Organ Archive	14	08	482-488
	ethnic history	19	01	8-15
		28	04	225-241
	Gloucestershire Record Office	19	01	8-15
	Guernsey	21	01	20-25
	guides and finding aids	06	02	45-48
		13	08	468-471
	Hertfordshire Record Office	03	06	253-256
	Isle of Man	22	02	74-83
	John Rylands Library	02	07	202-206
		19	02	71-73
	libraries and	08	06	205-211
	Lincolnshire	06	05	157-162

INDEX OF SUBJECTS

subject	sub-heading	vol	no	pages
archive services *(cont.)*	Liverpool	22	02	74-83
	local authority	23	02	98-102
	local government reorganisation	14	02	98-100
	Modern Records Centre (Warwick)	12	08	394-400
	National Register of Archives	01	04	127-129
	Norwegian	15	03	147-154
	opening hours	14	07	387-391
	publications by	13	06	341-345
		13	07	425-430
	Saffron Walden library	25	03	153-163
	St Deiniol's, Flintshire	23	01	40-44
	St Helena	28	02	108-122
	Scotland	09	07	353-356
		11	03	123-129
		14	02	98-100
	Scotland, National Library of	11	08	445-448
	Scottish National Portrait Gallery	11	07	382-384
	Scottish National Register of	01	12	374-377
	Scottish Record Office	11	03	123-129
	Sheffield	22	02	74-83
	Shropshire	26	03	168-174
	Spain	24	02	91-101
	Sussex record offices	12	06	267-273
	users	15	01	3-5
		22	02	74-83
		23	02	98-102
	Wales	13	06	341-345
	West Riding deed registry	15	05	277-287
	William Salt Library (Stafford)	19	03	114-116
	Yorkshire Archaeological Society	19	04	170-173
archive sources	see also *archives (general) ; bibliographies; and headings for individual categories of documents*			
	agricultural unions	13	05	259-262
	auction (sale) catalogues	13	03	131-139
	bankruptcy records	24	01	4-14
	black history	19	01	8-15
	British & Foreign School Society	16	04	204-206
	bus services	13	05	280-289
	business records	01	05	140-145
		06	04	128-133
		12	08	394-400
	canals and navigations	06	01	8-10
	cemetery records	28	03	130-144
	census, records of	05	08	260-269
	charters	17	02	71-77
	Chartism	03	01	11-19
	Christian (Plymouth) Brethren	14	08	478-481
	Church Building Commissioners	09	05	215-221
	Church Building Society	27	02	91-105
	Church Commissioners	09	05	215-221
	church courts	02	02	50-53
		04	01	12-22

subject	sub-heading	vol	no	pages
archive sources *(cont.)*	church history	07	01	17-27
	church records	25	01	7-16
	civil registration	03	03	108-112
	civil registration Scotland	03	03	108-112
	Civil War	26	04	194-208
	coal-mining	08	08	272-281
		18	01	5-12
	colleges of education	20	01	20-23
	commissary courts (Scotland)	17	01	4-10
	conciliar courts	04	03	89-94
	Congregationalism	03	05	208-212
	co-operative movement	09	04	163-171
	courts of equity	17	07	408-416
		17	08	475-482
	cutlers of Hallamshire	25	04	194-208
	diaries	25	03	130-141
	Ecclesiastical Commissioners	09	05	215-221
	enclosure records	05	07	218-220
		07	08	265-274
		12	01	18-25
		29	01	14-24
	Exeter Corporation	16	05	289-297
	family and estate records	19	02	71-73
		19	04	170-173
		25	04	231-241
		26	02	66-79
	farm records	12	08	407-420
		13	05	270-276
	field-names	13	07	388-396
	fire insurance records	09	01	3-8
		17	03	141-149
	friendly societies	16	03	161-167
		24	04	229-242
	further education	20	01	20-23
	guild records	09	06	267-274
	holiday resorts	13	06	323-331
	house histories	07	06	182-189
	immigrant communities	28	04	225-241
	income tax 1803	13	06	332-338
	industrial history	02	05	146-148
	inns and public houses	06	01	18-21
	inns of court	05	03	72-76
	juvenile delinquency	13	02	74-78
	Lancaster	21	02	60-65
	land tax	15	02	86-92
	lead-mining	18	03	112-118
	Leeds LEA	21	04	162-167
	legal records	04	08	307-314
	library records	15	07	406-413
	licensed trade	25	01	31-42
	local government	14	02	98-100
	Luddite activity	28	01	24-35

subject	sub-heading	vol	no	pages
archive sources *(cont.)*	manorial records	01	03	82-89
		15	03	166-173
		18	01	16-18
	medical practitioners	23	03	163-169
	medieval boroughs	02	11	321-325
		29	04	194-211
	Methodist	03	03	143-149
	military records	01	07	205-208
	modern records	12	08	394-400
	naval records	01	11	325-330
	New Poor Law	16	02	93-100
	newspaper industry	16	08	479-482
	nonconformity	08	04	131-134
	oral history	14	05	284-288
	overseers' records	14	01	11-17
	pamphlets, broadsheets	25	02	66-76
	parish records	06	04	110-114
	parks departments	20	04	158-165
	parliamentary constituencies	13	07	416-424
	parliamentary records	04	06	219-226
		04	07	267-274
		04	08	307-314
		04	08	354-358
	patent records	09	06	275-279
	petty sessions	15	02	74-79
	photographs	13	01	22-36
		15	08	468-473
	photographic surveys	09	05	222-225
	police forces	02	04	106-110
	poll taxes	03	07	371-278
	Poor Law Union	02	01	11-15
	poor law case study	16	01	15-20
	poverty, records of	25	01	17-30
	probate records	01	09	265-268
		15	08	478-482
	property deeds	10	01	7-12
	public health records	14	04	202-210
	Quaker records	08	07	258-262
		21	02	70-75
	quarter sessions records	08	01	22-27
	Queen Anne's Bounty	09	05	215-221
	railway records	01	03	90-94
		05	01	17-22
	recusant history	15	05	288-295
	regimental records	04	04	143-152
	retailing history	29	03	167-182
	rural settlement	15	08	456-463
	school managers' records	10	06	277-281
	school records	01	08	230-233
		17	08	490-493
		18	01	21-22
		29	02	102-113

subject	sub-heading	vol	no	pages
archive sources *(cont.)*	school records (Scotland)	17	01	11-18
	Scotland 17th c	15	08	456-463
	shipping records	05	06	177-182
	shop tax records	14	06	348-351
	Society of Friends	03	02	55-61
		21	02	70-75
	suburban development	04	07	275-281
		15	05	259-271
	taxation records	28	02	66-77
	teacher training	12	03-04	161-166
	temperance movement	08	04	135-138
	theatrical records	06	01	22-24
	tithe records	01	12	361-364
		07	08	265-274
		17	04	205-211
	trade union	01	09	273-277
		04	05	177-181
	trades councils	03	04	160-165
	transport records	04	08	329-334
	twentieth century	20	03	109-117
	unrest 18th century	04	06	235-241
	vernacular architecture	12	05	235-240
	village libraries	19	04	147-158
	village reading rooms	20	04	155-157
	women's history	23	02	92-97
	Welsh	07	05	154-160
		07	06	189-191
	workhouse records	10	02	70-75
archives (general)	see also *archive services; archive sources; libraries*			
	access policies	14	07	387-391
		14	08	451-453
		21	01	11-15
	calendaring, transcribing	25	01	7-16
	CD-ROM	24	02	83-90
	charging for access	14	07	387-391
		14	08	451-453
		15	01	24
	computerisation	25	04	209-222
	copying documents	02	10	311-312
		05	03	77-79
	early preservation	06	05	157-162
	ecclesiastical	05	02	44-50
	family portraits	06	03	74-78
	forged	03	03	105-107
	handling documents	02	10	311-312
	historical databases	20	02	88-99
	illustrations	05	05	151-154
	linguistic analysis	28	04	217-224
	local collections	21	01	11-15
	local government reform	16	05	278-281
	local historian and	13	04	217-223
		15	01	3-5

subject	sub-heading	vol	no	pages
archives (general) *(cont.)*	loss of	14	02	98-100
	microform copying	04	04	162-164
	organisation of records	06	02	45-48
	opening hours	14	07	387-391
	photographic	01	10	293-296
	photographing	15	04	229
	preservation of records	03	07	283-285
	publication of	08	07	237-242
	record linkages	27	02	78-90
	regional variability	18	03	136-141
	retention policies	19	03	120-123
	security issues	18	01	21-22
	survival of	14	01	11-17
	use in schools	07	02	47-52
		19	01	16-17
	users of	15	01	3-5
		22	02	74-83
		23	02	98-102
	VCH use of	22	03	128-137
armed forces	ancestors in	01	07	205-208
army records		04	04	143-152
		06	06	192-197
		13	08	475-480
art history	carving on fonts	23	03	130-145
	ceramics	24	01	37-43
	fine arts, sources	14	07	419-427
	graveyard sculpture	23	02	66-84
	war memorials	26	04	209-222
Artificers, Statute of		08	08	293-299
atheism	local history of	08	06	221-227
auction catalogues	local history value	13	03	131-139
autobiography	trade union leaders	13	05	259-262
	working class	12	03-04	131-135
baths	public	25	03	142-152
battlefields	marking of	01	12	371-374
	Stamford Bridge	04	02	84-85
bee-keeping	early history	29	03	130-151
bibliographies	agricultural history	09	07	323-333
		19	01	18-20
	agriculture	04	04	154-156
	Anglo-Saxon charters	17	02	71-77
	architecture	01	04	102-106
	architecture, vernacular	17	02	78-84
	biographies	14	07	419-427
	book trade	24	02	102-111
	castles	04	03	95-97
	children	17	04	219-225
	coaching services	14	06	341-346
	coal industry	08	08	272-281
	co-operative movement	09	04	163-171
	county maps	08	05	167-179
	court rolls	10	02	83-87

subject	sub-heading	vol	no	pages
bibliographies *(cont.)*	Dark Ages	02	03	72-75
	demography (urban)	10	03	142-146
	demography (Welsh)	10	06	291-294
	dialect	24	03	164-173
	diaries	14	04	211-221
		15	07	414-431
	Domesday Book	17	01	39-44
	early Britain	01	07	209-212
	early guidebooks	05	06	183-188
	education history	06	05	171-174
		09	03	130-134
		10	03	124-126
	electronic	19	03	117-119
	enclosure maps/awards	07	08	265-274
	enclosure (parliamentary)	12	01	18-25
	engineering	04	06	245-250
	engravings and prints	10	07	355-360
	estate maps and plans	07	07	223-231
	estate maps (Scotland)	12	01	26-30
	family histories	14	04	211-221
		14	07	419-427
	feet of fines	24	02	66-82
	food and drink	04	08	315-319
	geography	03	07	286-291
	gravestones	23	02	66-84
	house histories	14	07	419-427
	industrial archaeology	12	06	296-303
	industrial history	04	06	245-250
		14	07	419-427
	inns of court	05	03	72-76
	landscape history	14	04	195-201
		16	08	483-488
	local history 1978	13	05	262-270
	local history writing	12	06	277-283
		14	04	211-221
		15	07	414-430
	maps and plans	07	06	196-208
		07	07	223-231
		07	08	265-274
		08	02	61-71
		12	01	26-30
	marine charts	08	03	86-97
	medical history	16	01	32-35
	medieval Britain	01	04	106-112
	medieval court rolls	10	02	83-87
	medieval settlement	16	05	260-265
	medieval Wales	17	05	264-268
	military history	01	04	102-106
		16	07	405-411
	monasticism	01	04	102-106
	music history	11	06	315-320
		14	07	419-427

INDEX OF SUBJECTS

subject	sub-heading	vol	no	pages
bibliographies *(cont.)*	naval	01	11	325-330
	newspaper history	16	08	479-482
	oral history	15	07	414-431
	palaeography	16	06	327-334
	parliamentary constituencies	13	07	416-424
	parliamentary enclosure	12	01	18-25
	party politics	02	03	65-68
	place-names	17	07	396-404
	politics 18th century	23	02	103-110
	Poor Law	12	05	206-211
	population 18th c	10	03	142-146
	population history	16	04	207-212
	population (Wales)	10	06	291-294
	pottery industry	08	03	78-85
	property law	04	01	26-27
	public houses	08	04	126-130
	railway history	08	01	10-15
	recusant history	09	06	283-289
	religious history	08	07	237-242
		09	02	65-74
		09	06	283-289
		16	03	151-155
	religious census 1851	27	04	194-217
	Roman period	01	07	209-212
	rural settlement	07	01	7-13
	Russo, David	19	01	21-26
	St Helena	28	02	108-122
	Scottish	01	12	374-377
	settlement, medieval	16	05	260-265
	small buildings	07	03	92-94
	social history	12	03-04	131-135
	social history (Wales)	11	08	449-451
	suburban development	04	07	275-281
	tithe records	07	08	265-274
	town history	01	10	308-311
	towns and trade	08	06	196-204
	transport history	04	03	116-119
	travellers' accounts	03	01	20-31
		03	02	63-66
		08	06	196-204
	Tudor courts (law)	04	03	89-94
	urban growth	09	04	190-195
	urban history	16	02	67-72
	urban population 18th c	10	03	142-146
	vernacular architecture	17	02	78-84
	Victoria County Histories	13	01	15-22
	Wales, medieval	17	05	264-268
	Wales post-1536	17	06	358-365
	Welsh demography	10	06	291-294
	Welsh local history	09	01	16-22
	Welsh social history	11	08	449-451
	Welsh topography	11	01	7-13

subject	sub-heading	vol	no	pages
bibliographies *(cont.)*	women's history	17	03	150-157
	Yorkshire (East)	19	03	117-119
bigamy		24	03	139-144
biographical studies	bibliography of	14	07	419-427
	deposition evidence	17	05	269-276
	local history and	06	02	38-44
	organisation of	06	05	163-165
	publishing autobiography	27	04	218-224
biography	Barker, Thomas	15	02	70-72
	Biscoe, John	08	05	160-166
	Dictionary of Labour Biography	14	04	232-233
	Foster, Canon C.W.	06	05	157-162
	Hine, Reginald Leslie	07	01	28-32
	Hoskins, W.G.	22	04	170-183
	Hutton, William	04	06	251-254
	local history sources	25	03	130-141
	Merton College tenants	28	01	16-23
	nurse children	19	03	100-106
	Pevsner obituary	15	08	454-455
	printers and booksellers	24	02	102-111
	Quakers	21	02	70-75
	Russo, David	19	01	21-26
	Shakespeare, William	07	02	42-46
	trade union leaders	13	05	259-262
bishops' registers		07	01	17-27
bishops' returns		15	03	155-156
bishops' visitations		02	01	19-22
Black Death		05	03	85-89
Blake Report		14	06	325-331
		14	07	392-399
		15	01	3-5
	reactions to	14	01	18-23
		14	02	91-92
	summary of contents	13	08	451-456
Blue Books	trade union history	04	05	177-181
Bodleian Library		02	05	130-133
book trade	bibliographical index	24	02	102-111
	pre-1850 Cheshire	26	04	237-245
	probate evidence	15	08	478-482
books	husbandries	13	04	195-204
	library collections	19	02	58-62
		19	04	147-158
	literacy 16th/17th c	11	01	14-17
	ownership 17/18th c	15	08	478-482
	parish libraries	15	07	406-413
boroughs	accounts	02	10	293-296
	records	02	09	265-267
		29	04	194-211
	regional variation in density	29	04	194-211
botanical history	dumbles [rushes]	11	02	63-67
	hedgerow dating	17	06	327-342
	hedgerows	13	04	195-204

INDEX OF SUBJECTS

subject	sub-heading	vol	no	pages
boundaries	charters	01	08	241-245
		13	04	209-216
		27	01	18-29
	county	01	11	340-343
	early administrative units	15	08	483-485
	farms and estates	03	07	292-298
	field	03	01	1-8
	legislation concerning	04	02	67-72
	markers	18	02	58-64
	Ordnance Survey mapping	15	08	483-485
	origins of	01	11	340-343
	parish	01	11	340-343
		03	01	1-8
		14	05	262-269
		15	01	34-40
		18	02	58-64
	perambulation of	25	02	88-94
	pre-Conquest estates	27	01	18-29
	study areas	13	01	1-11
		29	04	256-262
brass	probate inventories	17	02	85-100
brasses, church		01	05	159-162
brewing		25	01	31-42
		29	04	194-211
bridges	see also *roads and highways*			
		07	08	250-252
	boundary markers	18	02	58-64
	Bristol	25	02	66-76
British Agricultural History Society		15	03	157-160
British and Foreign School Society		16	04	204-206
British Association for Local History		22	02	74-83
	county organisations survey	22	02	89-96
British Museum		02	01	1-3
British Optical Association		02	11	330-333
British Records Association		03	07	283-285
British Transport Commission		04	08	329-334
British Union of Fascists		27	02	106-117
Builder, The		12	07	353-359
building materials	cottages	01	12	365-367
	glebe terrier evidence	08	02	47-53
	general	07	04	126-132
building plans		19	03	120-123
	beerhouses	17	08	457-464
building registers		12	07	353-359
building societies	early development	10	02	65-69
building styles		02	04	106-110
building styles	vernacular	16	06	323-326
building trade	women workers	20	02	84-87
buildings	see also *architecture; and separate entries for individual types/categories*			
	all-electric house(1935)	28	02	94-107
	architects	21	02	60-65
	archive sources	02	04	106-110

subject	sub-heading	vol	no	pages
buildings *(cont.)*	auction catalogues	13	03	131-139
	barns	27	02	66-77
	baths, public	25	03	142-152
	bibliography	07	03	92-94
		17	02	78-84
	building plans	19	01	3-7
		19	03	120-123
	castles	04	02	62-64
		04	03	95-97
	changing styles	18	04	183-186
	chapels	21	01	4-10
	chimneys	01	08	252-255
	churches	02	01	15-18
		07	02	53-59
		07	01	17-27
	church restoration	21	03	120-125
	church towers	08	08	282-287
	cinemas	20	03	118-122
	cottage architecture	01	12	365-367
		10	07	327-332
	country houses	15	04	195-203
	craftsmen and domestic architecture	21	02	60-65
		07	04	126-32
	fire hazards	10	08	395-397
	fire insurance plans	11	06	343-349
	fire insurance records	09	01	3-8
	general	01	01	9-12
		01	06	187-190
	graffiti evidence	23	01	4-19
	Gothic architecture	02	07	197-201
	Great Rebuilding	14	02	68-75
	hearth tax evidence	11	07	385-389
	historic houses	25	04	223-230
	historical research	02	04	106-110
		07	06	182-189
		12	08	391-394
		15	01	6-20
	hospitals	24	01	15-26
	house recording	15	01	6-20
	hunting lodges	26	02	66-79
	Lincoln Cathedral	24	02	83-90
	masons' marks	02	08	232-234
	mills	02	06	172-175
	moated sites	05	02	34-38
		10	03	135-138
		11	02	89-93
	model farms	12	08	407-420
	parsonage houses	08	02	47-53
	public houses	25	01	31-42
	seaside attractions	24	04	194-205
	terrier evidence	01	12	361-364
	timber framing	27	02	66-77

INDEX OF SUBJECTS

subject	sub-heading	vol	no	pages
buildings *(cont.)*	title deeds	06	03	86-90
	Tudor quantity surveying	22	01	41-42
	vernacular architecture	12	02	81-84
		12	05	235-240
		16	06	323-326
		17	02	78-84
	watermills	02	11	326-329
	windmills	01	02	43-47
Buildings of England		15	08	454-455
bus services	charabanc traffic 1920s	24	04	217-224
Business Archives Council		06	04	128-133
business history	see also *commerce and trade; finance and accounting; industrial history; retailing; taxation and rates; and headings for individual businesses, trades or industries*			
	archives	12	08	394-400
	bankruptcies	24	01	4-14
	book trade	24	02	102-111
	business communities	11	08	457-464
	cemeteries	28	03	130-144
	collieries	08	08	275-281
	directory evidence	17	06	343-350
	fire insurance records	09	01	3-8
	general	06	04	128-133
	John Rylands Library	02	07	202-206
	methodology	01	05	140-145
	penny capitalism	17	04	226-235
	philanthropy	27	03	144-162
	rate books	17	05	277-280
	sequestration records	24	01	4-14
	shop tax	14	06	348-351
	sources for	01	05	140-145
	taxation 18th c	28	02	66-77
	tourist accommodation	24	04	217-224
	trade directories	13	04	205-209
	trades and crafts	28	03	145-158
	transport archives	04	08	329-334
	women traders 18th c	17	03	158-162
bus services	before 1930	15	04	221-224
	local history of	13	05	280-289
calendars		03	02	66-69
calendars of inquisitions		05	07	224-230
Calthorpe estate		15	05	259-271
Cambridge Group for History of Population		06	06	198-203
		07	06	178-181
		20	02	88-89
canals and navigations	company archives	04	08	329-334
	maps and plans	08	02	61-71
	projects of 1699	26	02	102-114
	research topics	07	03	84-87
	societies	02	09	257-260
	sources (general)	06	01	8-10
	Yorkshire Ouse	26	02	102-114

INDEX OF SUBJECTS

subject	sub-heading	vol	no	pages
cannon-making	Walkers of Rotherham	17	04	236-241
carriers' services	in 18th c	15	06	338-344
	motor vehicles and	17	06	351-357
carrots	cultivation of	04	01	1-7
cars	early ownership	17	06	351-357
cartography	enclosure maps	07	08	265-274
	estate maps and plans	05	03	66-71
		07	07	223-231
	estate plans (Scotland)	12	01	26-30
	local historians and	17	03	135-140
	maritime charts	08	03	86-97
	military encampment surveys	29	04	212-222
	Ordnance Survey	05	05	130-140
		05	07	202-211
		05	08	251-259
	OS historical maps	05	06	166-172
	surveyors 18th c	23	04	218-227
	tithe maps	07	08	265-274
	topographical maps	03	03	115-120
	village plans	09	05	233-241
castles and fortifications		04	02	62-64
		05	02	34-38
Catholicism	bibliography	09	06	283-289
	bishops' returns	15	03	155-156
	priest-holes	06	08	266-269
	recusant history	15	05	288-295
	registration of oaths	02	11	337-339
	religious census 1851	27	04	194-217
	religious returns 1829	17	08	483-489
cattle-droving		19	04	162-166
cemeteries	early 19th century	28	03	130-144
census data	see also *census returns; censuses; computing; family and kinship; population and demography; population mobility; research techniques*			
	analysis	01	06	174-177
		01	06	174-177
		05	08	260-269
		08	01	2-10
		09	01	27-35
		10	05	259-264
		11	03	155-161
		12	02	93-101
		14	02	79-90
		22	04	184-190
		29	04	223-230
	anomalies in	13	08	481-487
	computer analysis	15	08	464-467
		16	05	266-277
		16	06	335-342
		16	08	451-456
		18	02	69-75
		26	02	89-101
		27	04	194-217

INDEX OF SUBJECTS

subject	sub-heading	vol	no	pages
census data *(cont.)*	group projects	08	01	2-10
	housing	18	03	106-111
	micro-studies	18	03	119-126
	Preston (Lancashire)	11	03	155-161
	reliability	08	01	2-10
		11	03	155-161
		11	07	375-381
		14	02	79-90
		22	04	184-190
		23	04	205-216
		29	04	223-230
	Sheffield (Yorkshire)	29	04	223-230
census returns	see also *census data; censuses; computing; research techniques*			
	anomalies in	13	08	481-487
	beerhouses	17	08	457-464
	children	05	08	260-269
	clergy enumerators	14	02	79-90
	community analyses	29	04	223-230
	economic indicators	14	02	79-90
	employment	20	03	109-117
	enumeration books	10	05	259-264
	enumerators	18	01	19-20
	enumerators' schedules	11	03	155-161
	farm sizes	26	01	16-35
	farming communities	27	03	130-143
	general description	11	03	155-161
	house repopulation	13	02	86-97
	housing definitions	19	02	56-57
	housing statistics	12	07	353-359
		18	03	106-111
	immigration analysis	12	02	74-79
	industrial settlements	18	03	119-126
	Irish migration	29	02	66-75
	migration evidence	26	04	223-236
	occupations and employment	11	02	85-88
		17	04	199-204
		28	03	145-158
	overcrowding	10	05	259-264
		16	03	156-160
		18	03	106-111
		29	02	66-75
	parish register data 1831	14	02	79-90
	population mobility	17	04	199-204
		21	03	109-119
	pre-1841	18	01	19-20
	regional variations	18	03	136-141
	relationship definitions	13	08	481-487
	rural change and	17	04	199-204
	rural settlement	07	01	7-13
		15	01	25-32
		18	02	69-75
	Society of Genealogists	22	02	68-73

INDEX OF SUBJECTS

subject	sub-heading	vol	no	pages
census returns *(cont.)*	tithe record linkages	13	02	86-97
	tourists in	24	04	217-224
	trades and crafts	28	03	145-158
censuses	see also *census data; census returns; computing*			
	1676 religious	04	05	182-184
	1831 census	14	02	79-90
	1851 religious	11	07	375-381
		27	04	194-217
	1891 census	22	04	184-190
	1975 private	12	02	93-101
	early	04	04	129-133
	early	06	05	146-150
	general review	05	08	260-269
	pre-1801	10	01	13-26
	pre-1841	18	03	106-111
chamberlains' accounts		02	10	293-296
Chancery proceedings		06	08	254-259
Chancery, courts of		17	07	408-416
		17	08	475-482
	mining disputes	18	03	112-118
chantry certificates		04	04	129-133
chapels	see also *churches*			
	accounts	15	01	41-43
	Catholic	15	05	288-295
	nonconformist	10	05	253-258
		21	01	4-10
	private	21	01	4-10
charcoal-burning		08	01	16-21
charity and philanthropy	almshouses	28	04	208-216
	Battersea	27	03	163-182
	bequests to poor	16	01	21-23
	Bristol 1816-17	25	01	17-30
	charitable bequests	15	04	225-226
	charity administration	21	04	147-155
	Charity Organisation Society	21	03	109-119
	church briefs	02	06	165-167
		15	06	345-354
	church-building	27	02	91-105
	clergy charities	11	08	465-469
	educational	24	03	145-152
	estate cottages	16	01	4-14
	friendly societies	03	03	95-101
		16	03	161-167
	New Lanark	06	04	118-120
	parliamentary records	04	08	307-314
	probate accounts	21	02	51-59
	Putney Royal Hospital	24	01	15-26
	Richmond Philanthropic Society	27	03	144-162
	social class of benefactors	27	03	144-162
	subscriptions to	21	04	147-155
	voting charities	21	04	147-155
Charity Organisation Society		21	03	109-119

INDEX OF SUBJECTS

subject	sub-heading	vol	no	pages
Charity Organisation Society *(cont.)*		21	04	147-154
		23	01	45
charm cures		03	06	237-248
charters	Anglo-Saxon	01	08	241-245
		13	04	209-216
		17	02	71-77
		27	01	18-29
	bibliographies	17	02	71-77
	borough (medieval)	02	11	321-325
		29	04	194-211
	boundaries	01	08	241-245
		13	04	209-216
	forged	03	03	105-107
		13	04	209-216
	general	01	02	47-51
	John Rylands Library	02	07	202-206
	place-name evidence	13	04	209-216
Chartist Land Plan		18	02	76-79
Chartists		03	01	13-19
		03	02	49-54
Cheshire Churches Project		20	02	80-83
Chetham's Library		20	01	31-36
children	see also *family and kinship; household composition*			
	apprenticeships	02	12	357-361
		14	07	400-406
		19	02	51-55
	bibliography	17	04	219-225
	census evidence	05	08	260-269
	clothing	29	01	3-13
	families 1945-1970	28	04	i-xvi
	foundlings	07	08	258-260
		29	01	3-13
		29	03	152-166
	juvenile delinquency 19th c	13	02	74-78
	nurse children	19	03	100-106
	oral history	13	07	408-416
	orphans	21	02	51-59
	paupers	20	01	9-19
	plaiting trade	19	03	107-113
	poor relief for	25	03	164-177
	school logbooks	14	08	471-476
	truce terms	11	08	441-444
chimneys		01	08	252-255
cholera		21	04	168-176
Christian names	gravestone evidence	13	03	149-159
	Latin forms	01	10	312-314
Christian Brethren	archives	14	08	478-481
chronicles	monastic	02	04	102-105
	town	12	06	285-292
chronology	see also *dating methods*			
	archaeological	02	05	141-144
	customs and traditions	02	06	176-180

INDEX OF SUBJECTS

subject	sub-heading	vol	no	pages
chronology *(cont.)*	measuring time	03	02	66-69
	sundials and scratchdials	17	08	465-474
Church Commissioners	records	09	05	215-221
church (grave) yards	see also *memorials and monuments; sculpture and carving*			
		06	07	229-233
		14	03	164-167
		23	02	66-84
	Scottish	23	02	66-84
	stonemasons	16	07	412-417
	survey techniques	13	03	149-159
church bands		06	02	48-54
church briefs		02	06	165-167
		15	06	345-354
churches	see also *architecture; buildings; chapels; memorials and monuments; religious history*			
	architecture	02	01	15-18
		07	02	53-59
	brasses	01	05	159-162
		10	07	340-343
	building history	07	01	17-27
	Catholic chapels	15	05	288-295
	Catholic monuments	15	05	288-295
	chapels	15	05	288-295
		21	01	4-10
	Cheshire Churches project	20	02	80-83
	church (grave) yards	06	07	229-233
		13	03	149-159
		14	03	164-167
		23	02	66-84
	church bands	06	02	48-54
	'clipping the church'	14	08	489
	cricket teams	25	02	95-108
	floating barge church	16	07	431
	fonts	23	03	130-145
	furnishings	05	04	107-110
		07	08	253-257
		22	04	203-207
		23	03	130-145
		27	02	91-105
	glossary	02	01	15-18
	guides	20	02	80-33
		10	07	344-350
	historical sources	07	01	17-27
	Incorporated Church Building Soc	27	02	91-105
	inventories of goods	07	07	219-222
	liturgy and architecture	07	02	53-59
	medieval benefactions	28	01	3-15
	medieval Bristol	28	01	3-15
	medieval graffiti	23	01	4-19
	memorials and monuments	02	10	297-303
		02	12	362-365
		04	05	198-201

INDEX OF SUBJECTS

subject	sub-heading	vol	no	pages
churches *(cont.)*	memorials and monuments *(cont.)*	05	04	107-110
		06	02	48-54
		06	07	229-233
		16	07	412-417
		23	02	66-84
	music	06	02	48-54
		14	08	482-488
	organs	14	08	482-488
	parish magazines	16	08	457-466
	plate and vestments	07	07	219-222
	rates for repewing	22	04	203-207
	Reformation, consequences of	07	08	253-257
	round towers	08	08	282-287
	sculpture and carving	24	02	83-90
	seating	04	01	12-22
		11	07	375-381
		22	04	203-207
		27	02	91-105
	sports teams	25	02	95-108
	Suffolk	08	08	282-287
	sundials and scratch dials	17	08	465-474
	Victorian restoration	21	03	120-125
		27	02	91-105
	wafer ovens	07	05	161-165
	Warwick rebuilding 1699	26	02	102-114
	Welsh chapel Carlton (Yorks)	26	04	223-236
churchwardens		06	04	110-114
	accounts	01	08	234-237
cinemas		20	03	118-122
Cinque Ports		02	07	207-211
Cistercians	as wool-traders	04	04	134-139
civil engineering	1699 notebook	26	02	102-114
civil registration	Scotland	03	03	108-112
	Society of Genealogists	22	02	68-73
	surname evidence	20	01	3-8
		20	02	65-72
		27	04	i-xx
civil unrest	18th c	04	06	235-241
	20th c	27	02	106-117
	medieval Derbyshire	15	07	388-401
	peasant revolts in France	11	04	188-199
	racist rioting	27	04	225-244
Civil War	archive sources	26	04	194-208
	economic causes	01	01	13-17
	gentry allegiances	26	04	194-208
	local impact	01	01	13-17
		22	03	138-143
		22	04	191-202
	probate accounts	21	02	51-59
	religious causes	01	01	13-17
	soldiers' experiences	02	09	261-264
clergy	chancery proceedings	06	08	254-259

subject	sub-heading	vol	no	pages
clergy *(cont.)*	charitable provision for	11	08	465-469
	conflict with gentry	21	03	120-125
	ejection of	01	02	59-61
	Foster, Canon C.W.	06	05	157-162
	graffiti signatures	23	01	4-19
	Lewin, Rev. Edmund	13	07	397-405
	local influence of	15	07	388-401
	post-Reformation	07	08	253-257
	religious census 1851	11	07	375-381
	terrier evidence	01	12	361-364
	welfare of	11	08	465-469
clothing and costume	children's	29	01	3-13
	clothing of poor	01	09	269-272
	medieval graffiti	23	01	4-19
	spectacles	02	11	330-333
	stocking knitting	28	01	24-35
	women traders 18th c	17	03	158-162
co-operative movement	bibliography and sources	09	04	163-171
	sources 20th c	20	03	109-117
coaching services	bibliography	14	06	341-346
	in 18th c	15	06	338-344
coal-mining	bibliography	08	08	272-281
	Durham coalfield	16	07	418-424
	estate management	23	04	188-198
	finances	23	04	188-198
	finances 18th c	14	03	156-163
	maps and plans	08	08	275-281
	markets 18th c	14	03	156-163
	photographs	16	05	298
	sources	18	01	5-12
	Yorkshire 19th century	23	04	188-198
	Yorkshire, South	16	02	73-82
coinage		02	01	1-3
		06	01	2-7
	Anglo-Saxon	25	01	3-6
colleges of education	see also *education (current); local history*			
	archives	20	01	20-23
	local history in	11	07	395-399
colonialism	St Helena	28	02	108-122
	status of immigrants	27	04	225-244
colonies	family history	01	04	117-122
commerce and trade	see also *business history; finance and accounting; industrial history; industries; retailing*			
	agricultural marketing	13	05	270-276
	apprenticeships	08	07	232-236
	bankruptcies	24	01	4-14
	Beccles market	21	02	76-78
	borough rights and privileges	29	04	194-211
	boycott of German goods	27	02	106-117
	building trade	20	02	84-87
	business communities	11	08	457-464
	chancery proceedings	06	08	254-259

INDEX OF SUBJECTS

subject	sub-heading	vol	no	pages
commerce and trade *(cont.)*	coins and tokens	06	01	2-7
	corn trade	08	06	196-204
	craft guilds	09	06	267-274
	directory evidence	11	02	85-88
	freemen's rolls	09	02	89-95
	international trade	22	01	18-40
	late medieval decline	29	04	194-211
	lead trade	18	03	112-118
	licensed trade	17	08	457-464
		25	01	31-42
	local history of	06	04	128-133
	maritime	05	06	177-182
	medieval Bristol	28	01	3-15
	medieval exports	22	01	18-40
	medieval market towns	29	04	194-211
	medieval measures	06	04	115-117
	medieval overseas	28	01	3-15
	medieval timber trade	27	02	66-77
	medieval wool trade	22	01	18-40
	memoranda rolls	05	08	242-246
	merchant inventories	04	06	227-231
	merchant marks	05	04	98-106
	parliamentary records	04	08	307-314
	pawnbroking	20	01	24-30
	place-name evidence	07	05	146-149
	pottery industry	24	01	37-43
	quarter sessions evidence	08	06	196-204
	St Helena	28	02	108-122
	taxation records	28	02	66-77
	timber	20	02	73-79
	trade tokens	06	02	55-61
	urban growth	08	04	118-125
		08	06	196-204
		11	05	263-277
		29	04	194-211
	urban retailing	29	03	167-182
	wife-selling	06	06	188-191
	woollen trade	04	04	134-139
Commerce, Chambers of		16	01	36-48
commissary courts	testaments	17	01	4-10
commons		07	07	232-240
	boundaries	18	02	58-64
	encroachments on	11	03	141-147
Commons Registration Act 1965		07	07	232-240
community	definitions of	26	01	36-47
	identification of	29	04	223-230
community history	see also *local history; regional history*			
	American perspectives	19	01	21-26
	census analyses	29	04	223-230
	community facilities	16	05	supp
	conflict in 19th c	21	03	120-125
	David Russo's writing	19	01	21-26

subject	sub-heading	vol	no	pages
community history *(cont.)*	development of	12	02	67-73
	entertainments	16	05	supp
	industrial colonies	23	03	146-154
	local history and	06	04	121-124
		06	06	182-185
	micro-studies	18	03	119-126
	oral history and	10	07	334-339
	parish magazines	16	08	457-466
	recent publications (1983)	15	07	414-431
	review article	09	07	357-361
	total approach	10	08	398-401
	validity of	14	07	392-399
		29	04	256-263
	Welsh in Yorkshire	26	04	223-236
	writing projects	13	05	276-280
Compton Census 1676		04	05	182-184
computer imaging	cathedral sculpture	24	02	83-90
computing	see also *census data; census returns; research techniques*			
	census analysis	15	08	464-467
		16	05	266-277
		16	06	335-342
		16	08	451-456
		18	02	69-75
	conference	20	03	126-127
	data analysis	11	08	452-456
		16	06	335-342
		23	01	20-30
		25	04	209-222
	databases	16	05	266-277
		16	08	451-456
		24	02	102-11
		25	02	77-87
		25	04	194-208
		25	04	209-222
		26	02	89-101
		29	01	43-51
	enclosure studies	25	02	77-87
	general review	23	01	20-30
		25	04	209-222
	historical databases	20	02	88-89
	local history uses (1974)	11	03	129-133
	methodologies	26	02	89-101
	probate inventory analysis	12	05	228-234
	religious census 1851	27	04	194-217
	rural settlement analysis	18	02	69-75
	simulation exercises	19	02	63-70
	surname distribution	27	04	i-xx
conference reports	computing in local history	20	03	126-127
	CORAL 1980	14	05	270-275
	landscape history	25	02	109-115
	Manchester 1994	25	04	242-244
	Warwick 1995	26	03	175-177

subject	sub-heading	vol	no	pages
Congregationalism		03	05	208-212
conservation	cathedral sculpture	24	02	83-90
	common land protection	07	07	232-240
	country houses	26	02	80-88
	historic landscapes	13	08	456-467
	industrial archaeology	09	06	289-293
	Ironbridge Museums	09	06	289-293
	local history and	11	07	400-405
	photographs	01	10	293-296
	rural landscapes	26	02	80-88
	town interpretation	12	05	204-206
Conservative Party		02	03	65-68
	Bexley (Kent)	11	05	285-289
	Richmond (Surrey)	27	03	144-162
	women supporters	28	03	159-175
constables	accounts	01	11	335-339
	parish	01	02	38-42
		04	08	325-328
		06	04	110-114
construction industry	women workers	20	02	84-87
conveyancing	title deeds	06	03	86-90
copyright	archives	05	03	77-79
	definitions	08	03	106-108
Conference of Regional and Local Historians		14	05	270-275
		28	03	176-179
councillors	social status	19	04	159-161
counties	abolition of metropolitan	16	05	278-281
	administrative maps	05	08	251-259
	archives	16	05	278-281
	Civil War administration	22	04	191-202
		26	04	194-208
	county councils	23	01	31-39
	local administration	26	03	130-141
	lords lieutenant	26	03	130-141
	taxation and rates	12	01	7-12
	unit of study	29	04	256-262
	Victoria County Histories	13	01	15-22
		22	03	114-127
counting systems		14	05	282-283
		15	01	21-23
countryside	access issues	07	07	232-240
county history	Cussan's *Hertfordshire*	03	06	253-256
	Gentleman's Magazine	16	06	346-350
	Lincolnshire project	09	03	111-114
	validity of	29	04	256-262
court rolls		04	03	98-100
		10	02	83-87
Courtauld Institute		07	02	59-62
courts	see also *archive sources; crime and punishment; law and order; legal system; manorial history*			
	archives of	04	08	354-358
	bankruptcy	24	01	4-14

subject	sub-heading	vol	no	pages
courts *(cont.)*	beerhouse licensing	17	08	457-464
	borough	16	05	289-297
	Chancery	01	02	47-51
		06	07	235-242
		06	08	254-259
		17	07	408-416
		17	08	475-482
	church	02	02	50-53
		02	08	245-246
		04	01	12-22
		07	01	17-27
		17	05	269-276
		21	03	120-125
		25	01	7-16
	church briefs	02	06	165-167
	common pleas	01	01	5-8
	criminal studies	16	05	289-297
	early	03	06	231-236
	equity	17	07	408-416
		17	08	475-482
	feet of fines	24	02	66-82
	general	05	07	224-30
		07	03	88-91
	inns of	05	03	72-76
	inquisitions post mortem	01	03	77-81
		06	07	235-242
	kirk sessions	11	04	229-233
	local 19th c	14	08	454-459
	manorial	02	12	374-375
		04	03	98-100
		07	01	2-7
		10	02	83-87
		14	02	93-97
	petty sessions	15	02	74-79
	Prerogative Court of Canterbury	14	04	222-225
	probate	01	09	265-268
		11	02	68-71
		12	01	36-37
		14	04	222-225
	quarter sessions	08	06	196-204
		12	01	7-12
	registration of oaths	02	11	337-339
	Scotland	03	08	329-331
	Star Chamber	04	03	89-94
		17	07	408-416
	Tudor conciliar	04	03	89-94
crime and punishment	see also *courts; law and order; police*			
	bigamy	24	03	139-144
	Bristol riots 1793	25	02	66-76
	child prisoners	15	06	366
	church courts	04	01	12-22
		25	01	7-16

INDEX OF SUBJECTS

subject	sub-heading	vol	no	pages
crime and punishment (cont.)	drunkenness	25	01	31-42
	early procedures	03	06	231-236
	Exeter 19th c	16	05	289-297
	game laws 19th c	26	03	142-154
	Gentleman's Magazine	15	02	80-84
	juvenile delinquency	13	02	74-78
	kirk sessions	11	04	229-233
	local studies	14	08	454-459
	Luddites	28	01	24-35
	petty offences	15	02	74-79
	poaching	14	04	226-232
	popular unrest	03	02	49-54
		04	06	235-241
		07	08	253-257
	Princes in the Tower	04	07	300-301
		05	01	7-8
	probate accounts	21	02	51-59
	racial discrimination	19	01	8-15
		27	04	225-244
		28	04	225-241
	rural crime 18th and 19th c	14	04	226-232
	rural unrest	03	02	49-54
	sentencing patterns	16	05	289-297
	servants, offences by	02	11	334-336
	social trends and	14	08	454-459
	sources for	16	05	289-297
	statistics of crime	14	08	454-459
	urban crime	16	05	289-297
	vagrancy	02	10	309-311
		21	02	66-69
crops	experimental	23	02	85-91
	introduction	04	01	1-7
	inventory evidence	16	04	217-227
		17	02	85-100
curriculum	see also *education (current); local history; schools*			
	local history in	06	07	218-222
		06	07	223-224
		06	07	225-227
		11	06	331-334
		12	05	223-228
		12	08	403-407
		15	04	204-211
		18	04	174-182
		19	01	16-17
		21	03	126-130
customs and excise	archives	02	07	207-211
	medieval trade	22	01	18-40
customs and traditions	see also *folk history; myths and legends*			
		01	01	9-12
		05	07	224-30
	almanacs	03	02	66-69
	beating the bounds	25	02	88-94

INDEX OF SUBJECTS

subject	sub-heading	vol	no	pages
customs and traditions (cont.)	church music	06	02	48-54
	clipping the church	14	08	489
	counting systems	14	05	282-283
		15	01	21-23
	demography and	06	05	146-150
	Denmark	05	07	221-224
	folk medicine	03	06	237-248
	folk memories	09	06	300-303
	folk names	11	02	63-67
	folk songs	04	05	185
		09	07	343-347
	funerals	23	04	199-204
	graffiti	23	01	4-19
	hatchments	02	05	138-140
		05	05	145-150
		06	05	169-170
	industrial	11	02	72-76
	inheritance (Scotland)	17	01	4-10
	inheritance patterns	26	01	16-35
	legends	06	04	134-135
	May Day celebrations	04	07	296-299
	merchant marks	05	04	98-106
	open-air courts	03	06	231-236
	public health	05	03	85-89
	rag-wells	15	03	177
	stone carving	16	07	412-417
	traditional furniture	18	04	168-173
	truce terms	11	08	441-444
	use in dating	02	06	176-180
	valentine cards	09	03	134-141
cutlery trade	Hallamshire	25	04	194-208
		29	04	223-230
databases	census analysis	16	08	451-456
	computing	16	05	266-277
		24	02	102-11
		25	02	77-87
		25	04	194-208
		25	04	209-222
		26	02	89-101
		29	01	43-51
	management of	26	02	89-101
	occupations and employment	16	05	266-277
	war memorial recording	26	04	209-222
dating methods	archival	02	06	176-180
	calendars and almanacs	03	02	66-69
	customs and traditions	02	06	176-180
	hedgerow dating	13	04	195-204
		14	01	28-33
		17	06	327-342
	regnal years	01	01	23-26
		02	06	176-180
	saints' days	01	06	182-185

INDEX OF SUBJECTS

subject	sub-heading	vol	no	pages
death	embalming of corpses	23	04	199-204
	gravestone evidence	13	03	149-159
	intervals before burial	23	04	199-204
	oral history	13	07	408-416
	paupers	20	01	9-19
	probate accounts	21	02	51-59
debts	inventory evidence	16	04	217-227
deer parks	Bolton Priory estate	26	02	66-79
defamation	church courts	25	01	7-16
demography	see *census; family and kinship; population and demography*			
deposition books		17	05	269-276
depositions	church courts	25	01	7-16
Derby Mercury	farm sale advertisements	28	01	36-49
Deserted Medieval Village Research Group		02	07	193-196
deserted villages		02	07	193-196
		13	08	471-474
	Nidd (Yorkshire)	28	04	208-216
dialect	bibliographies	24	03	164-173
	counting systems	14	05	282-283
		15	01	21-23
	folk-names	11	02	63-67
	pre-industrial England	14	07	407-410
	truce terms	11	08	441-444
diaries	agricultural apprentice [anon]	12	03-04	139-145
	analysis of	09	06	294-299
	bibliography	14	04	211-221
	Cecil, James	07	04	108-109
	Dunn, Matthias	16	07	418-424
	Harrold, Edmund	20	01	31-36
	Jackson, Rev Edward	26	01	36-47
	Quaker	21	02	70-75
	recent publications (1983)	15	07	414-431
	soldiers'	04	04	143-152
	source material	25	03	130-141
	topographical description in	10	01	27-32
Dictionary of Labour Biography		14	04	232-233
diocesan records	see also *archive sources; courts; probate records; religious history*			
	bishops' licences	05	01	2-6
	bishops' returns	15	03	155-156
	church courts	04	01	12-22
	church history	07	01	17-27
	citations	15	06	355-357
	general	02	03	82-86
		05	02	44-50
		06	05	157-62
		07	01	17-27
	Wales	07	05	154-160
diocesan visitations		15	06	355-357
directories, trade	see also *business history; commerce and trade; finance and accounting; industrial history; urban history*			
		18	04	187-189
		21	03	109-119

subject	sub-heading	vol	no	pages
directories, trade *(cont.)*	business communities	11	08	457-464
	coaching services	14	06	341-346
	evidence for retailing	29	03	167-182
	industrial growth and	13	06	349-352
	industrial structure	12	03-04	152-156
	market towns	11	02	85-88
	pawnbroking businesses	20	01	24-30
	reliability	13	04	205-209
		13	06	349-352
		15	03	144-146
		17	06	343-350
	rural trades and crafts	28	03	145-158
disease and illness	see also *doctors; health and medical care; hospitals; population and demography; public health*			
		29	02	102-113
	bibliography	16	01	32-35
	cholera	21	04	168-176
	demography of	06	05	146-150
	dispensaries in 19th c	10	05	221-226
	doctor's casebook 18th c	20	04	173-186
	heredity and	01	01	18-23
	insanity	21	02	51-59
	medical care	20	04	173-186
	medieval England	05	03	85-89
	oral history	13	07	408-416
	plague	14	06	332-340
	probate accounts	21	02	51-59
	public health	14	04	202-210
	treatment of incurables	24	01	15-26
	treatments 18th c	20	04	173-186
	typhoid Lincoln 1905	14	03	142
dispensaries	Victorian	10	05	221-226
district councils	councillors	19	04	159-161
doctors		23	03	163-169
	in 18th c	20	04	173-186
	inventories	04	08	320-324
	licensing	05	01	2-6
Domesday Book		01	09	261-264
		01	10	297-300
		01	11	344-347
	bee references	29	03	130-151
	bibliography	17	01	39-44
	facsimile edition	17	02	107-108
	parish/township units	27	01	3-17
	place-names	07	05	146-148
Domesday Survey 1910		16	05	282-283
Dr Williams's Library		09	03	115-120
drains and sewers		02	02	33-36
ducking stools		03	06	231-236
East India Company		01	04	117-122
Ecclesiastical Commissioners		09	05	215-221
ecclesiastical census 1676		04	05	182-184

INDEX OF SUBJECTS

subject	sub-heading	vol	no	pages
economic history	see *agricultural history; agriculture; business history; commerce and trade; industrial history; industries; occupations and employment; retailing; taxation and rates; trades and crafts; urban history*			
education (current)	see also *curriculum; local history; schools*			
	adult education	02	01	8-11
		10	08	385-389
	archives in schools	07	02	47-52
		19	01	16-17
	archive teaching packs	13	07	425-430
	churchyards as resource	06	07	229-233
	colleges of education	11	07	395-399
	further	20	01	20-23
		21	04	162-167
	group projects	24	01	28-35
	local history (US)	15	04	204-211
	local history classes	06	06	182-185
		22	02	58-67
	local history in	06	01	11-17
		06	07	218-222
		06	07	223-224
		06	07	225-227
		11	06	331-335
		12	05	223-228
		12	08	403-407
		13	03	140-145
		13	05	290-296
		13	08	451-456
		18	04	174-182
		21	03	126-30
	museums	04	06	242-244
	school history exhibition	02	05	149-150
	school records	17	08	490-493
	university local history	13	02	67-80
Education Act 1902		15	08	474-477
education history	see also *libraries; literacy*			
	administrative methods	21	04	162-167
	agricultural communities	15	08	474-477
	archives	18	01	21-22
		21	04	162-167
	bibliography	06	05	171-174
		09	03	130-134
		10	03	124-126
	British and Foreign School Society	16	04	204-206
	charity schools	24	03	145-152
	church records	05	02	44-50
	church records (Scotland)	17	01	11-18
	citations	15	06	355-357
	county councils	23	01	31-39
	further education	20	01	20-23
	informal 16th c	11	08	473-476
	inventory evidence	04	08	320-324
	literacy	21	01	16-19

subject	sub-heading	vol	no	pages
education history *(cont.)*	literacy 17th c	11	01	14-17
		14	03	134-141
	mechanics' institutes	07	02	63-65
	medieval chronicles	02	04	102-105
	New Lanark	06	04	118-120
	open air schools	29	02	102-113
	oral evidence 1945-1970	28	04	i-xvi
	parish libraries	15	07	406-413
	parliamentary records	04	08	307-314
	reformatories	13	02	74-78
	religious instruction	24	03	145-152
	school administration	15	03	137-143
	school boards	09	03	130-134
		10	06	277-281
	school histories	01	08	230-233
		02	05	149-150
	school logbooks	14	08	471-476
	school managers	10	06	277-281
	school records	04	01	29-33
		17	08	490-493
	Scotland	17	01	11-18
	straw-plaiting schools	19	03	107-113
	teacher training 19th c	12	03-04	161-166
	Victorian libraries	25	03	153-163
	Victorian schoolmasters	15	03	137-143
	village libraries	19	02	58-62
		19	04	147-158
	village reading rooms	20	04	155-157
elections	county council	23	01	31-39
	franchise changes 1867	13	07	416-424
	hustings	14	06	359
	in 18th century	23	02	103-110
electoral registers		11	01	30-34
	regional variability	18	03	136-141
Electrical Association for Women		28	02	94-107
electricity industry		28	02	94-107
Elementary Education Act 1870		09	03	130-134
emigration	to Quebec	04	01	9-11
enclosure	acts and awards	05	07	218-220
	bibliography	07	08	265-274
		12	01	18-25
	commissioners	29	01	14-24
	common land	07	07	232-240
	computer analysis	25	02	77-87
	Derbyshire 17th c	28	04	194-207
	disputes in 16th c	15	07	388-401
	emparking process	28	04	208-216
	field-names	02	12	353-356
	land sales at	12	07	337-341
	land tax returns	06	05	152-156
	legal disputes	29	01	14-24
	legal framework	14	06	352-357

INDEX OF SUBJECTS

subject	sub-heading	vol	no	pages
enclosure *(cont.)*	maps and awards	03	03	115-120
		07	08	265-274
	open fields, fossilised	04	02	73-77
	parliamentary	12	01	18-25
		29	01	14-24
		29	01	25-42
	poor people and	25	03	164-177
	Scottish records	07	08	265-274
	tithe evidence	01	12	361-364
	upland estates	26	02	66-79
	urban development and	10	03	126-134
	Victorian	01	06	178-181
	water supplies	26	03	155-167
	Welsh records	07	08	265-274
English Organ Archive		14	08	482-488
English Place Name Society		02	02	44-47
		07	05	146-149
		22	03	114-127
environmental issues	common land	07	07	232-240
	early conservation battle	24	03	153-163
	garden villages	27	01	30-47
	pollution 19th c	24	03	130-138
	resort amenities	24	04	217-224
equity, courts of		17	07	408-416
		17	08	475-482
estate accounts		25	04	231-241
estate management	see also *agricultural history; agriculture; farms; land ownership; landscape history; maps and plans; parks and gardens; rural settlement*			
	agricultural innovation	04	01	1-7
	Angus 17th c	15	08	456-463
	Bridgeman, Charles, as designer	06	03	91-96
	changes 19th c	03	07	292-298
	college accounts	28	01	16-23
	emparking	28	04	208-216
	enclosure	29	01	25-42
	enclosure land sales	12	07	337-341
	farm accounts	11	07	406-413
	fishponds	07	04	119-126
	game protection	26	03	142-154
	garden villages	27	01	30-47
	histories	14	07	419-427
	Holkham estate (Norfolk)	12	08	407-420
	long-term development	26	02	66-79
	manorial evidence	15	03	166-173
	manorial surveys	07	01	2-7
	maps and plans	03	03	115-120
		05	03	66-71
		05	03	66-71
		07	07	223-231
		12	01	26-30
	medieval	16	05	260-265
	medieval barns	27	02	66-77

subject	sub-heading	vol	no	pages
estate management *(cont.)*	medieval measures	06	04	115-117
	mineral exploitation	23	04	188-198
	model farms	12	08	407-420
	model villages	16	01	4-14
	ownership	02	08	230-231
	parks	03	08	332-349
	rabbits	18	01	13-15
		18	02	53-57
	suburban development	15	05	259-271
	surveying in 18th c	23	04	218-227
estate maps and plans		03	03	115-120
		05	03	66-71
		07	07	223-231
		12	01	26-30
		26	02	66-79
estate records	agricultural labourers	14	01	35-43
	Chetham's Library	20	01	31-36
	game books	25	04	231-241
	John Rylands Library	02	07	202-206
	vernacular architecture	12	05	235-240
	Wales	07	05	154-160
estate villages	workforce	14	01	35-43
estates	boundary charters	27	01	18-29
	pre-Conquest	12	06	273-277
ethnic history	Battersea early 20th c	27	03	163-182
	black people in Britain	19	01	8-15
	Indians in Leicester	28	04	225-241
	Jewish	27	02	106-117
	local history and	19	01	8-15
	methodology	20	02	59-64
	Muslim migration to NE	27	04	225-244
	oral history	20	02	59-64
	sources	19	01	8-15
		28	04	225-241
evangelism	religious tracts	10	03	116-124
Exchequer	court records	17	07	408-416
	memoranda rolls	05	08	242-246
exhibitions	19th century	26	01	3-14
	local history	01	01	30-33
	national and local 1851	09	05	233-241
	Northern Ireland	02	06	168-171
exploration		10	05	160-166
factories	architecture	09	04	183-189
fairs		08	06	196-204
	early modern	08	04	118-125
	May Day	04	07	296-299
	medieval	29	04	194-211
family and kinship	see also *children; family reconstitution; family linkages; genealogy; population and demography; population mobility*			
	1891 census	22	04	184-190
	agricultural labourers	27	03	130-143
	ancestral research	10	04	180-182

INDEX OF SUBJECTS

subject	sub-heading	vol	no	pages
family and kinship *(cont.)*	bigamy	24	03	139-144
	biographical data	06	05	163-165
	black families	20	02	59-64
	census anomalies	13	08	481-487
		29	04	223-230
	children's history	17	04	219-225
	compiling pedigrees	02	12	372-373
	computer linkages	25	04	209-222
	courtship evidence	17	05	269-276
	demography	06	05	146-150
	elite suburbia	15	05	259-271
	ethnic groups	19	01	8-15
	family history	14	05	259-261
	family reconstitution	06	05	146-150
		06	06	198-203
		09	01	9-15
		25	04	209-222
		27	02	78-90
	foundling children	07	08	258-260
	genealogy	02	02	37-40
		03	07	279-282
		04	02	56-61
		05	06	173-176
	General Strike	16	02	83-89
	genetics	01	01	18-23
		27	04	i-xx
	graveyard studies	14	03	164-167
	habitual territories	26	01	36-47
	heirlooms	16	04	217-227
	household size	27	03	130-143
	household structure	05	08	260-269
		12	02	93-101
		29	04	223-230
	inheritance patterns	26	01	16-35
	interracial marriages	27	04	225-244
	land market	26	01	16-35
	locational stability	15	03	132-134
	manorial customs	14	02	93-97
	manorial tenancies	15	03	166-173
	marriage	10	06	282-290
	marriage licences	10	06	282-290
	marriage patterns	27	04	225-244
		29	04	223-230
	matrimonial disputes	04	01	12-22
	midwifery	23	03	163-169
	mining families	16	07	418-424
	nurse children	19	03	100-106
	oral history	13	07	408-416
	oral history 1945-1970	28	04	i-xvi
	parish register evidence	26	01	36-47
	pauper beneficiaries	16	01	21-23
	plague contagion	14	06	332-340

subject	sub-heading	vol	no	pages
family and kinship *(cont.)*	portraits	06	03	74-78
	probate accounts	21	02	51-59
	probate issues	16	03	133-145
	proofs of age	05	07	224-230
	puritans	16	04	213-216
	record linkages	25	04	209-222
		27	02	78-90
	residence	02	04	106-110
	royal blood	01	06	166-169
	Shakespeare linkages	07	02	42-46
	Sheffield east enders in 19th c	29	04	223-230
	surname stability	12	01	3-6
	surnames	02	04	114-116
		20	01	3-8
		20	02	65-72
		27	04	i-xx
	war memorials	26	04	209-222
	Welsh genealogy	07	06	189-191
	wife-selling	06	06	188-191
family history	see *genealogy and family history*			
family reconstitution		06	05	146-150
		06	06	198-203
		09	01	9-15
		25	04	209-222
		27	02	78-90
	computer analysis	25	04	209-222
	record linkages	25	04	209-222
	record linkages	27	02	78-90
	validity of	29	04	256-262
farms	accounts	11	07	406-413
	auction catalogues	13	03	131-139
	notebooks	13	05	270-276
	plan and design	12	08	407-420
	probate inventories	12	05	228-234
	sales	09	07	334-337
		28	01	36-49
	size	12	02	88-92
		14	05	262-269
		26	01	16-35
		27	03	130-143
fascism	Bexley (Kent)	11	05	285-289
	in General Strike	16	01	36-48
	Scottish	27	02	106-117
fashion and taste	building styles	18	04	183-186
	early car ownership	17	06	351-357
	furniture	18	04	162-167
Fawcett Library	women's history	23	02	92-97
feet of fines		01	01	5-8
	bibliography	24	02	66-82
felons	associations for prosecution of	14	04	226-232
festivals	use in dating	02	06	176-180
field books		15	02	67-69

INDEX OF SUBJECTS

subject	sub-heading	vol	no	pages
field books	Domesday 1910	16	05	282-283
field-names		02	12	353-356
	land use evidence	26	02	66-79
	progress review	13	07	388-396
	Suffolk	17	05	285-289
	tithe maps	14	05	262-269
fields	bibliography	04	04	154-156
	enclosure 19th c	01	06	178-181
	enclosure patterns	29	01	14-24
	encroachments on waste	11	03	141-147
	estate maps and plans	05	03	66-71
		07	07	223-231
	hedgerows	17	06	327-342
	open fields	05	01	23-28
	open fields, fossilised	04	02	73-77
	patterns 19th c	03	07	292-298
		14	05	262-269
		29	01	14-24
	ridge and furrow	07	03	95-98
	terrier evidence	01	12	361-364
	tithe maps	14	05	262-269
fieldwork		09	04	183-189
	general discussion	03	01	1-8
	Roman roads	04	07	282-290
	surveying	05	04	115-120
final concords		14	07	411-416
finance and accounting	see also *accounts; business history; commerce and trade; taxation and rates*			
	bankruptcy sequestrations	24	01	4-14
	borough accounts	02	10	293-296
	building societies	10	02	65-69
	business accounts	21	02	76-78
	charity fundraising	27	03	144-162
	charity schools	24	03	145-152
	coal-mining	14	03	156-163
		23	04	188-198
	college accounts	28	01	16-23
	commissary court testaments	17	01	4-10
	constables' accounts	01	11	335-339
	debt and credit 17th c	28	04	194-207
	early textile industry	15	05	277-287
	estate accounts	11	07	406-413
		25	04	231-241
	fire insurance	09	01	3-8
		11	06	343-349
		17	03	141-149
	friendly society accounts	24	04	229-242
	highway surveyors	01	10	301-304
	household accounts	16	08	467-477
		26	01	36-47
	income tax 1803	13	06	332-338
	inventories of church goods	07	07	219-222
	manorial accounts	01	04	112-117

subject	sub-heading	vol	no	pages
finance and accounting (cont.)	market trading	21	02	76-78
	medieval prices	02	09	271-272
	medieval trade	22	01	18-40
	memoranda rolls	05	08	242-246
	minister's accounts	01	04	112-117
	monastic accounts	04	04	134-139
	monetary values	02	08	235-244
	money-lending in inventories	12	05	228-234
	overseers' accounts	01	09	269-272
		16	01	15-20
		20	01	9-19
	parson's accounts	13	07	397-405
	penny capitalism	17	04	226-235
	post-Reformation prices	02	10	304-308
	probate accounts	21	02	51-59
	probate inventories	16	04	217-227
	probate valuations	16	08	467-477
	regional income levels	13	06	332-338
	taxation 18th c	28	02	66-77
	wage regulation	08	08	293-299
fire	urban disasters	10	08	395-397
	insurance records	09	01	3-8
		11	06	343-349
		17	03	141-149
fishing industry	Whitby	28	02	78-93
fishponds		07	04	119-126
folk history	animal cures	03	06	237-248
folklore	industrial	11	02	72-76
	folk music 19th c	12	01	13-17
	folk songs	04	05	185
		05	05	141-144
		09	07	343-347
	folk songs Lancashire 19th c	12	01	13-17
	wife-selling	06	06	188-191
fonts		23	03	130-145
food and drink	archaeology	01	12	378-381
	bibliography	04	08	315-319
	cheese-making	13	05	270-276
	cooking equipment	04	04	157-161
	fishponds	07	04	119-126
	honey	29	03	130-151
	mead	29	03	130-151
	milk	13	05	270-276
	oral history	13	07	48-416
	probate accounts	21	02	51-59
	public houses 1930s	25	01	31-42
	starvation in General Strike	16	02	83-89
footpaths		01	03	73-76
forest law		03	07	305-307
forests, medieval		26	02	66-79
		28	04	194-207
foundlings		07	08	258-260

subject	sub-heading	vol	no	pages
foundlings *(cont.)*		29	01	3-13
		29	03	152-166
freemasonry		19	04	170-173
freemens' rolls		09	02	89-95
friendly societies		03	03	95-101
	archives	16	03	161-167
	finances	24	04	229-242
	rural communities	06	08	271-278
	sources	29	02	91-101
funeral customs	cemeteries	28	03	130-144
	England 17th c	23	04	199-204
	probate accounts	21	02	51-59
furniture and furnishings	all-electric house (1935)	28	02	94-107
	dressing furniture	18	04	162-167
	inventory evidence	02	03	76-79
		04	04	157-161
		16	03	133-145
		16	04	217-227
	urban 17th c	20	03	128-136
	Victorian	18	04	168-173
gallows and gibbets		03	06	231-236
game laws		26	03	142-154
garage businesses		17	06	351-357
garden cities	Stirling smallholdings	17	01	31-38
Garden Cities Association		27	01	30-47
gardens and parks		03	08	332-349
	auction catalogues	13	03	131-139
	Charles Bridgeman	06	03	91-96
	deer parks	26	02	66-79
	Georgian town houses	14	02	68-75
	inventory of Kip engravings	04	01	23-25
	landscaping	25	04	231-241
	pleasure gardens	03	08	319-324
	relict hedgerows	18	02	65-68
	Repton, Humphrey	03	08	332-349
	Sherborne Castle	25	04	231-241
	terminology	09	08	394-398
	Victorian development	20	04	158-165
	village destruction	28	04	208-216
	Weston-super-Mare	20	04	158-165
gas industry		23	04	188-198
gavelkind		26	01	16-35
Genealogists, Society of		01	03	70-73
		22	02	68-73
genealogy and family history		01	01	18-23
		01	03	70-73
		04	02	56-61
		05	06	173-176
	army ancestors	01	07	205-208
	beginning	03	07	279-282
	bibliography	14	04	211-221
	biographies	14	07	419-427

subject	sub-heading	vol	no	pages
genealogy and family history *(cont.)*	civil registration	03	03	108-112
	civil registration (Scotland)	03	03	108-112
	elusive ancestors	10	04	180-182
	family history	14	05	259-261
	gravestones	23	02	66-84
	habitual territories	26	01	36-47
	heraldry	01	08	238-241
	Indian	01	04	117-122
	local history and	06	02	38-44
	nature of	14	05	259-261
	naval ancestry	01	11	325-330
	parliamentary records	04	07	267-274
	pedigrees, compiling	02	12	372-373
	popularity	07	06	178-181
	pre-1538	10	05	227-233
	pre-Conquest	02	02	37-40
	probate records	01	09	265-268
	proofs of age	05	07	224-230
	publications	14	07	419-427
	recent developments	07	06	178-181
	regional societies	13	02	100-102
	review article	09	07	357-361
	royal blood	01	06	166-169
	surnames	20	01	3-8
		20	02	65-72
	Welsh	07	06	189-191
		25	03	178-185
General Register of the Poor		17	01	19-30
General Strike		16	01	36-48
		16	02	83-89
genetics	family history	01	01	18-23
	surname distribution	27	04	i-xx
Gentlemans' Magazine		25	03	130-141
	in 18th c	15	02	80-84
	in 19th c	16	06	346-350
gentry	Civil War allegiance	22	03	138-143
		22	04	191-202
		26	04	194-208
	estate management	28	04	208-216
	local administrative role	22	04	191-202
	local councillors	19	04	159-161
	local politics 1918-45	28	03	159-175
	moated sites	05	02	34-38
	open and closed villages	06	08	271-278
	relationship with clergy	21	03	120-125
	lifestyles (inventories)	02	03	76-79
	local history and	03	07	286-291
glebe lands		01	12	361-364
glebe terriers		08	02	47-53
		12	05	235-240
glossaries	see also *bibliographies*			
	administrative units	27	01	3-17

INDEX OF SUBJECTS

subject	sub-heading	vol	no	pages
glossaries *(cont.)*	agriculture	04	04	152-153
		04	05	195-197
		04	07	291-295
	archaeological	02	05	145
	churches	02	01	15-18
	dialect	24	03	164-173
	fonts and their decoration	23	03	130-145
	Latin Christian names	01	10	312-314
	Latin, medieval	01	11	331-335
	Latin surnames	01	12	368-371
	legal terms	03	06	249-252
	manorial terms	01	03	86-89
	milling terms	02	06	175
	parochial records	01	04	122-124
	place-name elements	01	02	56-59
		22	03	114-127
	saints days	01	06	183-185
Goad, Charles E. (Ltd)	fire insurance	11	06	343-349
government (central)	see also *finance and accounting; parliament; politics; taxation and rates*			
	letters patent	01	02	47-51
	medieval accounting methods	22	01	18-40
	memoranda rolls	05	08	242-246
	political parties	02	03	65-68
government, local	see *local government; parish and township administration*			
graffiti	medieval	23	01	4-19
	Roman	02	10	289-292
gravestones	correspondence re	14	05	289-291
	inscriptions on	02	10	297-303
	probate accounts	21	02	51-59
	Roman inscriptions	02	10	289-292
	sculpture and carving of	06	07	229-233
		16	07	412-417
		23	02	66-84
	slate headstones	08	06	213-217
	survey techniques	13	03	149-159
Great Exhibition		09	05	241-245
Green Howards	military museum	14	02	76-78
guide books	18th and 19th c	05	06	183-188
	cemeteries 19th c	28	03	130-144
	churches	10	07	344-350
	country houses	15	04	195-203
	optimistic tone of	08	03	98-106
	travellers'	11	01	7-13
	Whitby	28	02	78-93
guilds	medieval borough	02	11	321-325
	medieval Bristol	28	01	3-15
	records	09	06	267-274
Gunpowder Plot		06	08	266-269
Guppy's surname survey		16	07	392-404
Hanse	merchants and traders	22	01	18-40
Harvard University	Shakespeare links	07	02	42-46
hatchments, funeral		02	05	138-140

subject	sub-heading	vol	no	pages
hatchments, funeral		05	05	145-150
(cont.)		06	05	169-170
health and medical care	see also; *doctors; hospitals; population and demography; public health*			
	animal cures	03	06	237-248
	bibliography	16	01	32-35
	charitable concern for	21	04	147-155
	cholera in 19th c	21	04	168-176
	demography	06	05	146-150
	dispensaries	10	05	221-226
	in 18th c	20	04	173-186
	licensing of doctors	05	01	2-6
	medieval England	05	03	85-89
	nurse children	19	03	100-106
	open air schools	29	02	102-113
	oral evidence 1945-1970	28	04	i-xvi
	oral history	13	07	408-416
	overcrowding	16	03	156-160
	paupers	01	09	269-272
	plague	14	06	332-340
	pollution 19th c	24	03	130-138
	Poor Law provision	20	01	9-19
	Poor Law, old	16	01	15-20
	provision for poor	10	05	221-226
	public baths	25	03	142-152
	Royal Hospital, Putney	24	01	15-26
	rural sanitation	21	04	156-161
	seaside holidays	24	04	206-216
	sources 19th c	14	04	202-210
	spectacles	02	11	330-333
	surgeons	23	03	163-169
	treatment of 19th c poor	10	05	221-226
	treatments 18th c	20	04	173-186
	water supplies	26	03	155-167
	women	23	02	92-97
Hearth Tax	population evidence	04	05	182-184
	settlement studies	11	07	385-389
	social structure from	28	04	194-207
	surname distribution	27	04	i-xx
hedgerows	see also *fields; landscape history*			
	dating	13	04	195-204
		14	01	28-33
		17	06	327-342
	enclosure	29	01	14-24
	historical development	13	04	195-204
	suburban relict	18	02	65-68
heraldry		02	08	235-237
	achievements	06	05	169-170
	bear and ragged staff	03	05	217-219
	church monuments	02	12	362-365
	civic	02	12	362-365
	genealogy and	01	08	238-241
	hatchments	02	05	138-140

subject	sub-heading	vol	no	pages
heraldry *(cont.)*	hatchments *(cont.)*	05	05	145-150
		06	05	169-170
	introduction	11	08	470-472
	merchant marks	05	04	98-106
Heralds, College of		02	12	362-365
heredity		01	01	18-23
heritage	see also *conservation; environmental issues; industrial archaeology*			
	archival	26	03	168-174
	Cheshire Churches project	20	02	80-83
	concept of 'country'	27	04	i-xx
	conference report	26	03	175-177
	country house guidebooks	15	04	195-203
	folk museums	03	05	197-207
	industrial archaeology	09	06	289-293
	industrial sites	02	08	225-229
		05	02	56-60
	Ironbridge Museums	09	06	289-293
	local history and	11	07	400-405
		24	04	225-228
		29	04	256-262
	management issues	26	02	80-88
	military museums	14	02	76-78
	National Trust	26	02	80-88
	National Trust for Scotland	25	04	223-230
	seaside resorts	24	04	194-205
	social elites in	25	04	223-230
	town interpretation	12	05	204-206
	Victorian concern for	26	01	3-14
	war memorial conservation	26	04	209-222
higher education	local history qualifications	16	07	388-391
historians and antiquarians	archive collections	20	01	31-36
	Bailey, John Eglinton	26	01	3-14
	Bede, Venerable	02	04	102-105
	Carus-Wilson, E.M.	22	01	18-40
	Chambers, J.D.	09	07	323-333
	Coleman, O.	22	01	18-40
	Cussans, John Edwin	03	06	253-256
	Dyos, H.J.	11	05	278-284
	Earwaker, John Parson	26	01	3-14
	Emmison, F.G.	26	02	115-116
	Ernle, Lord	09	07	323-333
	Finberg, H.P.R.	06	02	38-44
		11	05	306-307
		14	07	392-399
		21	03	99-108
		29	04	256-262
	Fitzhugh, Terrick	22	01	6-13
	Foster, Canon C.W.	06	05	157-162
	Hine, Reginald Leslie	07	01	28-32
	Hoskins, W.G.	06	02	38-44
		14	07	392-399
		21	03	99-108

INDEX OF SUBJECTS

subject	sub-heading	vol	no	pages
historians and antiquarians *(cont.)*	Hoskins, W.G. *(cont.)*	22	01	14-17
		22	03	144-146
		22	04	170-183
		29	04	256-262
	Hutton, William	04	06	251-254
	Kerridge, Eric	09	07	323-333
	Kuerden, Richard	20	01	31-36
	Marshall, J.D.	06	02	38-44
		06	06	182-185
		07	04	102-108
		14	06	325-331
		29	04	256-262
	Midgley, L. Margaret	22	04	209-212
	nature of	14	07	392-399
	Paris, Matthew	02	04	102-105
	Parker, Rowland	12	08	391-394
	Phythian Adams, Charles	21	03	99-108
		26	01	36-47
		29	04	256-262
	Raines, Francis R.	20	01	31-36
	Rawlinson, Richard	02	05	130-133
	Russo, David J.	19	01	21-26
	Skipp, V.H.	06	07	233-234
	Stenton, Sir Frank	25	01	3-6
	Thompson, F.M.L.	09	07	323-333
	Watkin, William Thompson	26	01	3-14
	Whitelock, Dorothy	25	01	3-6
	William of Worcester	03	01	1-8
		28	01	3-15
	Winchester, Angus J.L.	29	04	256-262
History & Computing, Association for		20	02	88-89
Hooper's hedgerow index		17	06	327-342
horseshoes		03	03	102-104
hospitals	charitable provision	21	04	147-155
	foundling	29	01	3-13
		29	03	152-166
	hospice 18th c	20	04	173-186
	Royal Hospital and Home, Putney	24	01	4-14
house repopulation		29	04	256-262
	Melbourn case study	13	02	86-97
		14	03	134-141
household composition		12	02	93-101
	census anomalies	13	08	481-487
		29	04	223-230
	census databases	16	05	266-277
	industrial communities	18	03	119-126
	Sheffield east end in 19th c	29	04	223-230
	urban poor	21	03	109-119
	Victorian suburbs	15	05	259-271
household goods	probate inventories	16	03	133-145
household size	census evidence	18	03	106-111
	change over time	18	03	119-126

INDEX OF SUBJECTS

subject	sub-heading	vol	no	pages
household size *(cont.)*	Sheffield metalworkers 19th c	29	04	223-230
housing	see also *architecture; buildings; census returns; public health*			
	auction catalogues	13	03	131-139
	bibliography	07	03	92-94
	building materials 18th c	08	02	47-53
	building registers	12	07	353-359
	building societies	10	02	65-9
	census 1891	22	04	184-190
	census definitions	18	03	106-111
		19	02	56-57
	census evidence	05	08	260-269
	church records	05	02	44-50
	clearance of	15	01	6-20
	contemporary journals	12	07	353-359
	cottages	01	12	365-367
		10	07	327-332
	country houses	15	04	195-203
	electricity supplies	28	02	94-107
	estate dwellings	28	04	208-216
	fire insurance records	17	03	141-149
	furnishings	04	04	157-61
	garden cities	17	01	31-38
	garden villages	27	01	30-47
	Georgian town houses	14	03	149-155
	hearth tax	11	07	385-389
	historical analysis	14	03	149-155
	historical research	02	04	106-110
		07	06	182-189
		15	01	6-20
	home ownership	28	04	225-241
	house repopulation	13	02	86-97
		14	03	134-141
	immigrant communities	28	04	225-241
		29	02	66-75
	industrial colonies	23	03	146-154
	inter-war	11	01	24-29
	inventories as source	04	04	157-161
		12	05	235-240
	Irish community	29	02	66-75
	Kip engravings	04	01	23-25
	land tax records	15	02	86-92
	local authority inter-war	11	01	24-29
	merchant marks	05	04	98-106
	miners' 19th c	24	03	130-138
	moated sites	05	02	34-38
	model communities	16	01	4-14
	MOH reports	12	07	353-359
	new towns 19th c	10	04	186-195
	New Lanark	06	04	118-120
	overcrowding	10	05	259-264
		16	03	156-160
		18	03	106-111

subject	sub-heading	vol	no	pages
housing *(cont.)*	overcrowding *(cont.)*	29	02	66-75
	parsonage houses	08	02	47-53
	planned communities	06	04	118-120
	poor law settlement	02	09	268-270
	poor, urban	08	03	98-106
	poor, 1820s	25	03	164-177
	poor, Edwardian	21	03	109-119
	private inter-war	11	01	24-29
	probate inventories	04	04	157-161
		12	05	235-240
	rateable values	15	05	259-271
	recording history	02	04	106-110
	recording of	15	01	6-20
	rural water supplies	26	03	155-167
	social segregation	11	01	30-34
	sources	14	03	149-155
	squatter encroachments	11	03	141-147
	suburban	15	05	259-271
	town houses	14	02	68-75
	vernacular architecture	16	06	323-326
housing associations	inter-war	11	01	24-29
	New Lanark	06	04	118-120
Hull University	local history degree	16	07	388-391
hundred rolls		05	01	9-16
		20	02	73-79
husbandry	legislation governing	02	11	334-336
hygiene	medieval	05	03	85-89
illegitimacy		17	01	19-29
immigration	see also *ethnic history; migration; population mobility*			
	black people in Britain	19	01	8-15
	German refugees 1930s	27	02	106-117
	Indians in Leicester	28	04	225-241
	Jewish (19th c)	27	02	106-117
	Muslim migration to NE	27	04	225-244
Imperial War Museum		26	04	209-222
	war memorial survey	20	03	123-125
income tax	returns 1803	13	06	332-338
Incorporated Church Building Society		27	02	91-105
indexes	agricultural history	19	01	18-20
	book trade	24	02	102-111
	post-1858 probate records	15	04	218-220
	techniques for making	17	05	281-284
Indian community	Leicester 1965-95	28	04	225-241
	NE merchant seamen	27	04	225-244
industrial archaeology		02	08	225-229
		12	06	296-303
	bibliography (Scotland)	12	06	296-303
	early factory sites	09	04	183-189
	early industrial sites	08	01	16-21
		09	02	85-88
	Ironbridge Museums	09	06	289-293
	recent progress	05	02	56-60

subject	sub-heading	vol	no	pages
industrial history	see also *business history; commerce and trade; industries; industrial relations; labour history; occupations and employment; trades and crafts*			
	archaeological evidence	09	02	85-88
	archaeology of factories	09	04	183-189
	archive sources	02	05	146-148
		12	05	241-245
		12	08	394-400
		20	01	31-36
	bibliography	14	07	419-427
	building plans	19	01	3-7
	business communities	11	08	457-464
	business histories	06	04	128-133
	census evidence	20	03	109-117
	company towns	15	07	388-401
	Durham miners	16	07	418-424
	early industrial sites	08	01	16-21
	early industrialisation	15	05	277-287
	early iron forges	09	02	85-88
	estate maps and plans	07	07	223-231
	fire insurance records	17	03	141-149
	folk music	12	01	13-17
	General Strike	16	01	36-48
		16	02	83-89
	industrial colonies	23	03	146-154
	industrial location	12	05	241-245
	industrial structures	12	03-04	152-156
	Ironbridge Museums	09	06	289-293
	labour migration	26	04	223-236
	literature as source	09	02	75-79
	medieval cloth trade	22	01	18-40
	modern industries	16	03	146-150
	New Lanark	06	04	118-120
	Nottinghamshire Luddites	28	01	24-35
	oral history and	14	05	284-288
	pauper apprentices	14	07	400-406
	place-name evidence	07	05	146-149
		08	01	16-21
	planned communities	06	04	118-120
	probate inventories	04	06	227-231
		16	03	133-145
	proto-industrialisation	27	02	78-90
	rate book evidence	17	05	277-280
	rural industries	08	07	232-236
		18	03	112-118
	structural changes	17	05	277-280
	timber resources	16	02	73-82
	trade directories	13	06	349-352
	trade unions	01	09	273-277
		04	05	177-181
		20	03	109-117
		27	02	106-117
		27	04	225-244

subject	sub-heading	vol	no	pages
industrial history *(cont.)*	trade unions *(cont.)*	28	03	159-175
	trades councils	03	04	160-165
	traditions and customs	11	02	72-76
	West Ham 20th c	20	03	109-117
	writing of	01	05	140-145
industrial relations	agricultural unions	11	03	134-141
		13	06	353-359
	Chartism	03	01	13-19
	coal-mining	16	07	418-424
	General Strike	16	01	36-48
		16	02	83-89
	lead-mining	18	03	112-118
	Leadhills strike 1836	17	02	101-106
industries	see also *industrial history; occupations and employment; trades and crafts*			
	brewing	25	01	31-42
		29	04	194-211
	cannon-making	17	04	236-241
	charcoal-burning	08	01	16-21
	cloth, medieval	22	01	18-40
	coal-mining	08	08	272-281
		14	03	156-163
		16	02	73-82
		16	07	418-424
		18	01	5-12
		23	04	188-198
		26	04	223-236
	coining	06	01	2-7
	construction and building	20	02	84-87
	cutlery	25	04	194-208
		29	04	223-230
	electricity supply	28	02	94-107
	fishing	28	02	78-93
	frame-knitting	28	01	24-35
	gas	23	04	188-198
	iron	08	01	16-21
		09	02	85-88
	ironstone-mining	16	02	73-82
	lead-mining	17	02	101-106
		18	03	112-118
		24	03	130-138
	lead-smelting	24	03	130-138
	leather trades	20	03	128-136
	milling	02	11	326-329
	paper-making	08	02	42-46
	pottery	08	02	54-60
		08	02	78-85
		24	01	37-48
	printing and engraving	24	02	102-111
		26	04	237-245
	quarrying	21	02	60-65
	rope-making	10	07	332-333
	salt	07	05	146-149

subject	sub-heading	vol	no	pages
industries *(cont.)*	silk	12	03-04	152-156
	steel-making	13	06	349-352
		29	04	223-230
	straw-plaiting	19	03	107-113
	woollen textiles	15	05	277-287
inheritance customs		15	03	166-173
inns and public houses	archive sources	02	05	134-137
		06	01	18-21
	beerhouses	17	08	457-464
	bibliography	08	04	126-130
	coaching services	14	06	341-346
	inter-war North East	25	01	31-42
	licensing	08	06	196-204
	naming	01	01	9-12
		12	01	31-35
		14	08	468-469
	photographs	16	08	489
	social role	02	05	134-137
	street-names from	16	04	195-203
	temperance movement	08	05	180-186
	urban growth 1570-1770	08	04	118-125
inns of court		05	03	72-76
inquisitions post mortem		01	03	77-81
		06	07	235-242
insanity	probate accounts	21	02	51-59
Institute of Historical Research		22	03	128-137
insurance	fire	09	01	3-8
		17	03	141-149
	fire (plans)	11	06	343-349
International Genealogical Index		19	02	63-70
		20	01	3-8
iron industry	archaeological evidence	09	02	85-88
	ironstone mining	16	02	73-82
	place-name evidence	08	01	16-21
Jackson's Oxford Journal		10	06	271-276
Jewish communities	Glasgow 1930s	27	02	106-117
Jewish faith	religious census 1851	27	04	194-217
John Rylands Library		02	07	202-206
		19	02	71-73
Journal of Transport History		04	03	116-119
justices of the peace		01	02	38-42
		08	08	293-299
		12	01	7-12
kirk sessions	registers	11	04	229-233
labour history	see also **industrial history; industrial relations; poverty; Poor Laws; trade unions**			
	agricultural trade unions	13	05	259-262
		13	06	353-359
	apprenticeships	02	12	357-361
		08	07	232-236
		17	05	269-276
		19	02	51-55

subject	sub-heading	vol	no	pages
labour history *(cont.)*	apprenticeships *(cont.)*	25	04	194-208
	archive sources	12	08	394-400
	Battersea politics	27	03	163-182
	biography	14	04	232-233
	Chartists	03	01	11-19
		18	02	76-79
	co-operative movement	09	04	163-171
	coal-mining	16	07	418-424
	craft guilds	09	06	267-274
	farm servants	02	11	334-336
	folk music	12	01	13-17
	friendly societies	03	03	95-101
	General Strike	16	01	36-48
		16	02	83-89
	industrial communities	29	04	223-230
	mechanics' institutes	07	02	63-65
	medical care	10	05	221-226
	migration	26	04	223-236
	Nottinghamshire Luddites	28	01	24-35
	oral evidence 1945-1970	28	04	i-xvi
	pauper mobility	12	03-04	136-139
	penny capitalism	17	04	226-235
	popular entertainments	09	08	379-386
	popular movements 18th c	04	06	235-241
	pub names	12	01	31-35
	radicalism and	25	01	17-30
	rural labour movements	03	02	49-54
	seaside holidays	24	04	194-205
	secularism and atheism	08	06	221-227
	self-help	10	02	65-69
		24	04	229-242
	strikes	11	03	134-141
		16	01	36-48
		16	02	83-89
		16	05	298
		16	07	418-424
		17	02	101-106
	trade councils	03	04	160-165
	trade unions	01	09	273-277
		04	05	177-181
		20	03	109-117
		27	02	106-117
		27	03	163-182
		27	04	225-244
		28	03	159-175
	wage assessments	08	08	293-299
	women and politics	28	03	159-175
	women, role of	28	02	94-107
	working-class racism	27	02	106-116
Labour Party	Battersea	27	03	163-182
	Bexley (Kent)	11	05	285-289
	early municipal	20	03	109-117

INDEX OF SUBJECTS

subject	sub-heading	vol	no	pages
Labour Party *(cont.)*	General Strike	16	02	83-89
	secularism and	08	06	221-227
	women supporters	28	03	159-175
lakes	industrial	09	02	82-88
Lambeth Palace Library		27	02	91-105
land holdings	Surrey 17th c	18	01	16-18
land market	feet of fines	24	02	66-82
	final concords	14	07	411-416
	Kent 19th c	26	01	16-35
	sales at enclosure	12	07	337-341
land owners	see also *estate management; gentry; land ownership; land tenure*			
	gifts to community	20	04	158-165
	private chapels	21	01	4-10
land ownership	see also *agricultural history; estate management; gentry; landscape history; land tenure; tenancy*			
	census returns	15	01	25-32
		27	03	130-143
	Chartists	18	02	76-79
	coal-mining	08	08	272-281
		18	01	5-12
	college estates	28	01	16-23
	conservation and	25	04	223-230
	Domesday 1910	16	05	282-283
	enclosure	29	01	25-42
	enclosure sales	12	07	337-341
	estate sizes	11	04	200-206
	farm sale evidence	28	01	36-49
	game laws	26	03	142-154
	garden villages	27	01	30-47
	hundred rolls	05	01	9-16
	land tax records	06	05	152-156
		15	02	86-92
		15	03	161-165
	landscape impact	28	04	208-216
	linguistics of sources	28	04	217-224
	local history and	06	02	38-44
	mineral revenues	23	04	188-198
	mortmain	09	08	387-394
	open and closed villages	06	08	271-278
	returns 1873	02	08	230-231
	smallholders	11	04	200-206
	social structure	15	01	25-32
		28	04	194-207
	sociology of villages	06	08	271-278
	street-naming	16	04	195-203
	suburban development	15	05	259-271
	tithe records	03	07	292-298
		12	02	88-92
	upland estates	26	02	66-79
	urban	15	02	86-92
	yeoman farmers	26	01	16-35
land sales	auction catalogues	13	03	131-139

INDEX OF SUBJECTS

subject	sub-heading	vol	no	pages
land tax		06	05	152-156
		07	06	182-189
		15	03	161-165
	rural settlement	07	01	7-13
	urban 18th c	28	02	66-77
	urban history and	15	02	86-92
	urban housing	14	03	134-141
land tenure	see also *estate management; land market; land ownership; tenancy*			
		01	01	5-8
		06	07	235-42
	bibliography	04	01	26-27
	charter evidence	01	08	241-245
	common land	07	07	232-240
	court rolls	04	03	98-100
	Domesday Survey	01	09	261-264
	enclosure	07	08	265-274
		12	07	337-341
	encroachments on waste	11	03	141-147
	estate maps and plans	05	03	66-71
	estate villages	14	01	35-43
	field book evidence	15	02	67-69
	final concords	14	07	411-416
	forest areas	03	07	305-307
	house histories	07	06	182-189
	hundred rolls	05	01	9-16
	inquisitions post mortem	01	03	77-81
	Kent 19th c	26	01	16-35
	land tax	15	02	86-92
		06	05	152-156
	lay subsidies	03	08	325-328
	legal views	14	06	352-357
	manor courts	04	03	98-100
	manorial customs	14	02	93-97
	manorial procedures	15	03	166-173
	manorial surveys	07	01	2-7
	middle-class yeomen	26	01	16-35
	mortmain	09	08	387-394
	ownership returns 1873	02	08	230-231
	plea rolls	01	05	155-158
	smallholdings	11	04	200-206
		17	01	31-38
	tithe evidence	12	02	88-92
	title deeds and leases	10	01	7-12
	village morphology	09	05	233-241
	Wales	07	05	154-160
landscape history	see also *agricultural history; enclosure; gardens and parks, land tenure; maps and plans; rural settlement; urban history*			
	aerial photography	15	07	402-405
	ancient routeways	12	05	212-220
	archaeology	03	04	153-159
		03	04	170-174
	auction catalogues	13	03	131-139

INDEX OF SUBJECTS

subject	sub-heading	vol	no	pages
landscape history *(cont.)*	battlefields	01	12	371-374
	bibliography	14	04	195-201
		16	08	483-488
	boundaries	15	08	483-485
	boundary charters	27	01	18-29
	boundary perambulations	25	02	88-94
	Bridgeman, Charles	06	03	91-96
	building societies	10	02	65-69
	cemeteries 19th c	28	03	130-144
	census returns	27	03	130-143
	chapels	21	01	4-10
	charters	01	08	241-245
		27	01	18-29
	church records	05	02	44-50
	coal-mining	23	04	188-198
	common land	07	07	232-240
	concept of 'country'	27	04	i-xx
	conference report	25	02	109-115
	conservation	13	08	456-467
		25	04	223-230
		24	03	153-163
	conservation 1920s	24	04	217-224
	Cornish agriculture	04	08	338-345
	county maps	08	05	167-179
	deer parks	26	02	66-79
	Derbyshire (North West)	28	04	194-207
	deserted villages	13	08	471-474
	Domesday evidence	01	11	344-347
	early industrial sites	09	04	183-189
	early industry	09	02	82-88
	emparking	28	04	208-216
	enclosure	07	08	265-274
		25	02	77-87
		29	01	14-24
		29	01	25-42
	enclosure and the poor	25	03	164-177
	encroachments on waste	11	03	141-147
	estate villages	16	01	4-14
		28	04	208-216
	farms 19th century	03	07	292-298
	feet of fines	24	02	66-82
	field books	15	02	67-69
	field patterns	04	02	73-77
	field surveys	05	04	115-120
	field-names	02	12	353-356
		13	07	388-396
		17	05	285-289
	final concords	14	07	411-416
	fishponds	07	04	119-126
	footpaths	01	03	73-77
	future development (1983)	15	06	323-332
	garden villages	27	01	30-47

INDEX OF SUBJECTS

subject	sub-heading	vol	no	pages
landscape history *(cont.)*	gardens	09	08	394-398
	general survey	15	06	323-332
	geography	03	07	286-291
	hedgerows	13	04	195-204
		14	01	28-33
		17	06	327-342
		18	02	65-68
	historic landscapes	13	08	456-467
	Hoskins, W.G.	14	04	195-201
	house recording	15	01	6-20
	Hutton, William	04	06	251-254
	images of cities 19th c	09	08	400-406
	Kings Lynn survey	08	04	139-145
	Kip engravings	04	01	23-25
	land law and	14	06	352-357
	landscape management	13	08	456-467
	Making of the English Landscape	02	11	347-350
		14	04	195-201
	maps and plans	03	03	115-120
		05	03	66-71
		07	07	223-231
	medieval Arden	07	04	119-126
	medieval Bristol	28	01	3-15
	moated sites	05	02	34-38
		10	03	135-138
		11	02	89-93
	model farms	12	08	407-420
	model villages	16	01	4-14
	monasteries	01	06	178-181
	open and closed villages	06	08	271-278
	Ordnance Survey maps	05	07	202-211
		05	08	251-259
		05	05	130-140
		05	06	166-172
	parish boundaries	15	01	34-40
	parks	03	08	332-349
		20	04	158-165
		25	04	231-241
	parks 18th c	09	02	82-88
	parliamentary records	04	07	267-274
	photography	20	04	166-172
	place-name evidence	22	03	114-127
	pleasure gardens	03	08	319-324
	pre-Conquest land-use	27	01	18-29
	rabbit warrens	09	02	59-64
	railways	03	05	191-197
	relict hedgerows	18	02	65-68
	Repton, Humphrey	03	08	332-349
	ridge and furrow	05	01	23-28
		07	03	95-98
	Roman roads	04	07	282-290
	rural housing	16	06	323-326

subject	sub-heading	vol	no	pages
landscape history *(cont.)*	street-names	16	04	195-203
	suburban development	04	07	275-281
	surveying in 18th c	23	04	218-227
	tithe maps	14	05	262-269
	topographical illustrations	07	02	59-62
	topographical place-names	12	06	273-277
	topographical poetry	17	03	163-168
	topographical surnames	27	04	i-xx
	topography 1770-1870	11	01	7-13
	town engravings	10	03	139-141
	town plans	07	06	196-208
	upland enclosure	26	02	66-79
	upland estates	26	02	66-79
	urban morphology	20	03	128-136
	urban parks	20	04	158-165
	VCH and	22	03	128-137
	Victorian environmentalism	24	03	153-163
	village morphology	09	05	233-241
	West Dean, Sussex	13	08	456-467
	woodland	16	02	73-82
		26	02	66-79
language and linguistics	counting systems	14	05	282-283
		15	01	21-23
	dialect terms, linguistics of	24	03	164-173
	folk-names	11	02	63-67
	Guernsey French	21	01	20-25
	linguistic analysis of sources	28	04	217-224
	newspapers 19th c	11	06	321-326
	place-name interpretation	13	04	209-216
	pre-industrial dialect	14	07	407-410
	truce terms	11	08	441-444
	use of by social classes	28	04	217-224
	Welsh (1891 census)	22	04	184-190
	Welsh (agricultural records)	07	05	154-160
	Welsh (among emigrants)	26	04	223-236
	Welsh (genealogical records)	07	06	189-191
	Welsh (place-names)	25	03	178-185
	Welsh (probate records)	25	03	178-183
Latin	Christian names	01	10	312-314
	inquisitions post mortem	01	03	79-81
		06	07	235-242
	letters patent	01	02	49-51
	medieval	01	11	331-335
	minister's account	01	04	114-116
	plea rolls	01	05	155-158
	surnames	01	12	368-371
	tripartite indenture	01	01	7
law and order	see also *courts; crime and punishment; legal system; police*			
	Bristol riots 1793	25	02	66-76
	church courts	02	02	50-53
		04	01	12-22
		25	01	7-16

subject	sub-heading	vol	no	pages
law and order *(cont.)*	crime studies	14	08	454-459
		16	05	289-297
	early controls	03	06	231-236
	game laws 19th c	26	03	142-154
	General Strike	16	01	36-48
		16	02	83-89
	juvenile delinquency	13	02	74-78
	Luddite activity	28	01	24-35
	parish constable	01	02	38-42
		01	11	335-338
		04	08	325-328
		06	04	110-114
	police records	02	04	111-113
	popular unrest 18th c	04	06	235-241
	private associations	14	04	226-232
	racist rioting	27	04	225-244
	rural labour unrest	03	02	49-54
	vagrancy	02	10	309-311
law enforcement associations		14	04	226-232
lawyers	enclosure work	29	01	25-42
	inventories for	04	08	320-324
lay subsidies		04	03	101-109
	population evidence	04	04	129-133
lead-mining	labour in coalfields	16	07	418-424
	strikes in	17	02	101-106
	Swaledale	18	03	112-118
lead-smelting	pollution	24	03	130-138
leases	probate evidence	16	04	217-227
leather industry	urban 17th c	20	03	128-136
legal disputes	lead-mining	18	03	112-118
legal history	Selden Society	01	07	220-224
legal system	see also *crime and punishment; courts; law and order; local government; manorial history; police*			
	archives	04	08	307-314
	bankruptcy	24	01	4-14
	beerhouse licensing	17	08	457-464
	borough courts	16	05	289-297
	borough privileges	29	04	194-211
	chancery	01	02	47-51
		06	07	235-242
		06	08	254-259
		17	07	408-416
		17	08	475-482
	church courts	02	02	50-53
		02	08	245-246
		04	01	12-22
		07	01	17-27
		17	05	269-276
		21	03	120-125
		25	01	7-16
	common pleas	01	01	5-8
	court archives	04	08	354-358

INDEX OF SUBJECTS

subject	sub-heading	vol	no	pages
legal system *(cont.)*	courts, general	05	07	224-30
		07	03	88-91
	crime studies	14	08	454-459
		16	05	289-297
	early procedures	03	06	231-236
	equity	17	07	408-416
		17	08	475-482
	forest law	03	07	305-307
	Guernsey	21	01	20-25
	inheritance law	14	06	352-357
	inquisitions post mortem	06	07	235-242
	judicial records	04	08	354-358
	juvenile delinquency	13	02	74-78
	manor courts	02	12	374-375
		04	03	98-100
		07	01	2-7
	mortmain, statute of	09	08	387-394
	probate	01	09	265-268
	probate procedures	16	04	217-227
	property law bibliography	04	01	26-27
	quarter sessions	08	06	196-204
	Scotland	03	08	329-331
	Star Chamber	04	03	89-94
		17	07	408-416
	terms used in	03	06	249-252
	title deeds	06	03	86-90
	Tudor courts	04	03	89-94
	Wales	25	03	178-185
Leicester School	local history in	06	04	121-124
		06	06	182-18
		06	07	233-234
		14	06	325-331
		21	03	99-108
	philosophy debated	29	04	256-262
leisure and entertainment	see also *music; seaside resorts; sport and recreation; theatre; tourism*			
	baths, public	25	03	142-152
	beerhouses	17	08	457-464
	cinemas	20	03	118-22
	civic ceremonial (Bristol)	28	01	3-15
	common land	07	07	232-240
	cricket	25	02	95-108
	drinking	25	01	31-42
	exhibitions of 1851	09	05	233-241
	family history and	14	05	259-261
	game shooting	26	03	142-154
	Henry VII in Bristol	28	01	3-15
	holiday visitors	13	06	323-331
	inland resorts	24	04	217-224
	inns and public houses	02	05	134-137
		06	01	18-21
		08	04	118-125
		08	04	126-130

subject	sub-heading	vol	no	pages
leisure and entertainment *(cont.)*	inns and public houses *(cont.)*	08	06	196-204
		25	01	31-42
	local history as	02	01	8-11
	local music history	11	06	315-320
	mass entertainment	03	08	319-324
	May Day	04	07	296-299
	middle-class	24	04	217-224
	military encampments 18th c	29	04	212-222
	music hall	09	08	379-386
	philanthropic societies	27	03	144-162
	pleasure gardens	03	08	319-324
	recreation rooms	16	05	supp
	seaside resorts	10	03	126-134
		24	04	194-205
		24	04	206-216
		28	02	78-93
	spa towns	10	04	186-195
	temperance events	08	05	180-186
	theatres	06	01	22-24
	tournaments	04	02	78-80
	Victorian parks	20	04	158-65
	visitors to resorts	23	04	205-216
letters	Civil War correspondence	22	03	138-143
	Gilbert, Sir Henry	23	02	85-91
	James, Cecil	07	04	108-109
	Lawes, Sir John	23	02	85-91
	postal services 18th c	29	03	152-166
	Lennard, Stephen	22	03	138-143
	soldiers'	04	04	143-152
letters patent		01	02	47-51
lexicography	local history	24	03	164-173
ley lines	debunking of	03	01	9-12
libraries	see also *archive services; archive sources; archives (general); education history; local history*			
	archive sources	15	07	406-413
	Bodleian	02	05	130-133
	Chetham's	20	01	31-36
	co-operative movement	09	04	163-171
	Congregationalism	03	05	208-212
	Dr Williams's Library	09	03	115-120
	Fawcett Library	23	02	92-97
	history	12	03-04	156-157
	Hull University	19	03	117-119
	Iron Acton village	19	04	147-158
	John Rylands	02	07	202-206
		19	02	71-73
	Lambeth Palace	27	02	91-105
	Leadhills	19	02	58-62
	local history and	08	06	205-211
	local studies collections	14	08	460-467
	Manx National	22	02	74-83
	National Library of Scotland	11	08	445-448

INDEX OF SUBJECTS

subject	sub-heading	vol	no	pages
libraries *(cont.)*	Northamptonshire	19	04	167-169
	parish	15	07	406-413
	parish packs	18	01	23
	Saffron Walden	25	03	153-163
	Shropshire Records & Res Centre	26	03	168-174
	Society of Genealogists	22	02	68-73
	Spain	24	02	91-101
	St Deiniol's	23	01	40-44
	village	19	02	58-62
		19	04	147-158
	William Salt	19	03	114-116
	Yorkshire Archaeological Society	19	04	170-173
lieutenancy	militia organisation	26	03	130-141
lighting	gas	11	06	327-330
Lincoln Record Society		06	05	157-162
literacy	see also *education history; libraries*			
	analysis of	21	01	16-19
	appraisers of inventories	16	03	133-145
	deposition evidence	17	05	269-276
	graffiti	23	01	4-19
	in 16th and 17th c	11	01	14-17
	language and	14	07	407-410
	ownership of books	15	08	478-482
	signature evidence	16	08	457-466
	sources 17th c	14	03	134-141
	village reading rooms	20	04	155-157
literature	as historical source	09	02	75-79
	bee-keeping references	29	03	130-151
	concept of 'country'	27	04	i-xx
	Gentleman's Magazine	15	02	80-84
	graveyards	06	07	229-233
	historical novels	08	07	243-250
	linguistic analysis	28	04	217-224
	local history source	06	02	38-44
		08	07	243-250
	poetry on war memorials	26	04	209-222
	suburban settings	04	07	275-281
	Thomas Hardy	06	02	48-54
	topographical poetry	17	03	163-168
	travellers' journals	03	01	20-31
	turnpike references	01	04	102-106
	Victorian evangelism in	10	03	116-124
	W.G. Hoskins, style of	22	04	170-183
livestock		04	05	186-195
		04	08	338-345
		17	02	85-100
	advertisements	28	01	36-49
	Cheshire 19th c	13	05	270-276
	Durham 19th c	17	04	205-211
	field-name evidence	17	05	285-289
	inventory evidence	12	05	228-234
		16	04	217-227

subject	sub-heading	vol	no	pages
local government	see also *counties; legal system; manorial system; parish and township administration; urban history*			
	administrative maps	05	08	251-259
	archive services	14	02	98-100
		23	02	98-102
	archive sources	02	09	265-267
	building control	12	07	353-359
	building plans	19	01	3-7
		19	03	120-123
	cemeteries	28	03	130-144
	Civil War administration	22	04	191-202
		26	04	194-208
	councillors	19	04	159-161
	county councils	23	01	31-40
	courts baron	02	12	374-375
	democratic procedures	27	03	163-182
	medieval	12	06	285-292
	medieval boroughs	29	04	194-211
	medieval Bristol	28	01	3-15
	Middlesex	23	03	155-162
	municipal socialism	27	03	163-182
	parish councillors	17	04	212-218
	parish politics	17	04	212-218
	parks and gardens	20	04	158-165
	police	02	04	111-113
		14	04	226-232
	police and watch	14	08	454-459
	public health functions	14	04	202-210
	Reading in 19th c	21	04	168-176
	regulation of retailing	29	03	167-182
	town meetings	27	03	163-182
local government reform		16	05	278-281
Local Historian	ex-editor's reflections	12	07	330-337
	history of	22	01	8-13
	publishing history	12	07	330-337
local history	see also *education (current); publishing local history; research techniques*			
	academic content	14	01	4-10
	academic development	10	08	385-389
	academic subject	26	01	3-14
		29	04	256-262
	adult education	02	01	8-11
		12	02	67-73
		12	06	267-273
	amateur in	06	01	11-17
		06	02	38-44
		06	04	121-124
		06	06	182-185
		06	07	233-234
		06	08	260-261
		10	08	385-389
		12	02	67-73
		14	06	325-331

subject	sub-heading	vol	no	pages
local history *(cont.)*	amateur in *(cont.)*	14	07	392-399
		15	06	333-337
		19	01	21-26
		22	01	14-17
		28	03	176-179
		29	04	256-262
	American perspectives	19	01	21-26
	Anglo-Saxon studies	25	01	3-6
	antiquarianism	06	08	260-261
		26	01	3-14
	approaches to	07	07	214-216
		29	04	256-262
	archives and	13	04	217-223
	Austria	11	04	207-217
	background to growth of	12	03-04	158-160
	bibliography 1978	13	05	262-270
	Blake Report	13	08	451-456
		14	01	18-23
		14	02	91-92
	boundaries of study	13	01	1-11
	British/US links	14	01	4-10
	C.O.R.A.L. and	28	03	176-179
	character of	25	01	43-44
		29	04	256-262
	church guides	10	07	344-350
	community history	06	04	121-124
		06	06	182-185
		12	02	67-73
		13	05	276-280
		26	01	36-47
	computing and (1974)	11	03	129-133
	computing, impact of	25	04	209-222
	country house visitors	15	04	195-203
	county organisations	11	04	225-228
		22	02	89-96
	curriculum subject	06	07	218-222
		06	07	223-224
		06	07	225-227
		11	06	331-334
		12	05	223-228
		12	08	403-407
		15	04	204-211
		18	04	174-182
		19	01	16-17
		21	03	126-130
	definitions	12	05	223-228
		14	06	325-331
		14	07	392-399
		15	08	486-489
		19	01	21-26
		29	04	256-262
	development of	10	08	390-394

subject	sub-heading	vol	no	pages
local history *(cont.)*	development of *(cont.)*	10	08	385-389
		15	06	333-337
		21	03	99-108
		22	01	8-13
		22	01	14-17
		22	04	170-183
		29	04	256-262
	exhibitions	03	01	39-42
		10	04	167-170
		26	01	3-14
	family history and	14	05	259-261
	fieldwork	03	01	1-8
	Finland	12	03-04	149-151
	group projects	22	02	58-67
		24	01	28-35
	Guernsey	21	01	20-25
	heritage movement	24	04	225-228
	Hoskins' contribution	22	03	144-146
		22	04	170-183
		29	04	256-262
	illustrated lectures	01	06	169-174
	in 19th century	26	01	3-14
	influence of media	15	06	333-337
	inter-disciplinary linkage	14	06	325-331
	Isle of Man	22	02	74-83
	Italy	11	05	251-262
	journals, scope of	07	04	102-108
	landscape history and	14	04	195-201
	Leicester School	06	04	121-124
		06	06	182-18
		06	07	233-234
		14	06	325-331
		21	03	99-108
		29	04	256-262
	library collections	14	08	460-467
	library resources	08	06	205-211
	Local Historian, The	12	07	330-337
		22	01	8-13
	methodology	03	01	1-8
		06	02	38-44
		22	01	14-17
		23	01	20-30
		29	04	256-262
	models	14	06	325-331
		21	03	99-108
	name of	15	08	486-489
	national dimensions	23	02	103-110
	new directions	12	02	67-73
		22	01	14-17
	Northern Ireland	12	03-04	167-168
	Norway	11	04	217-224
	philosophy	06	01	11-17

subject	sub-heading	vol	no	pages
local history *(cont.)*	philosophy *(cont.)*	06	02	38-44
		06	04	121-124
		06	06	182-185
		06	07	233-234
		06	08	260-261
		10	08	390-394
		13	01	1-11
		14	01	4-10
		14	07	392-399
		14	06	325-331
		15	06	333-337
		19	01	21-26
		21	03	99-108
		22	01	14-17
		25	01	43-44
		28	03	176-179
		29	04	256-262
	popularity	12	03-04	158-160
	professional in	06	01	11-17
		06	02	38-44
		06	04	121-124
		06	06	182-185
		06	07	233-234
		06	08	260-261
		10	08	385-389
		12	02	67-73
		14	06	325-331
		14	07	392-399
		15	06	333-337
		22	01	8-13
		28	03	176-179
		29	04	256-262
	publishing trends	12	07	330-337
	purpose debated	06	01	11-17
		06	02	38-44
		06	04	121-124
		06	06	182-185
		06	07	233-234
		06	08	260-261
		07	04	102-108
		13	01	1-11
		22	01	14-7
		23	01	20-30
		26	01	36-47
		28	03	176-179
		29	04	256-262
	qualifications	13	08	451-456
		16	07	388-391
	regional history and	12	05	223-228
		13	01	1-11
		14	06	325-331
		21	03	99-108

INDEX OF SUBJECTS

subject	sub-heading	vol	no	pages
local history *(cont.)*	regional history and *(cont.)*	26	01	36-47
		29	04	256-262
	research procedures	14	01	4-10
	resources for	15	01	3-5
	retrospective (1978)	12	07	330-337
	scale of sources	12	02	67-73
		22	02	89-96
	Scotland	09	07	353-356
		11	03	123-129
	social sciences and	10	08	390-394
	societies	01	07	202-205
		03	03	126-129
		12	06	267-273
		14	03	131-133
		15	08	491-492
		22	02	58-67
		22	02	89-96
		26	01	3-14
		29	04	256-262
	sociology, influence of	26	01	36-47
	sources 20th c	20	03	109-117
	Spanish	24	02	91-101
	spatial units	21	03	99-108
		29	04	256-262
	structure	14	01	18-23
	Sussex	12	06	267-273
	teaching in schools	06	07	218-222
		06	07	223-224
		06	07	225-227
		13	03	140-145
		13	05	290-296
		22	02	58-67
	title of *Amateur Historian*	07	03	78-83
	topographical writing	11	01	7-13
	total history of communities	10	08	398-401
	undergraduate courses	13	02	67-80
	United States	14	01	4-10
	Wales	09	01	16-22
		10	08	404-411
	Workers Education Association	10	08	385-389
London Gazette	local history uses	15	04	212-217
Loughton Mutual Labor-Aid Society		24	04	229-242
Luddites		28	01	24-35
machinery, agricultural		09	04	178-183
Magna Carta		03	07	305-307
Making of the English Landscape		02	11	347-350
		14	04	195-201
manorial history	see also *courts; land ownership; land tenure; legal system*			
	architectural records	12	05	235-240
	archive sources	07	06	182-189
	bees and honey	29	03	130-151
	bibliographies	10	02	83-87

subject	sub-heading	vol	no	pages
manorial history *(cont.)*	bibliographies *(cont.)*	16	05	260-265
	court rolls	04	03	98-100
		10	02	83-87
	courts	02	12	374-376
		07	01	2-7
	customs and procedures	14	02	93-97
		15	03	166-173
	economic development	29	04	194-211
	equity, courts of	17	07	408-416
	field books	15	02	67-69
	fishponds	07	04	119-126
	hundred rolls	05	01	9-16
	industrial development	25	04	194-208
	leases	10	01	7-12
		18	01	16-18
	local administrative role	27	01	3-17
	manorial organisation	01	03	82-85
	markets (medieval)	29	04	194-211
	planting on dunes	28	04	242-244
	property records	10	01	7-12
	social structure	01	03	82-85
	sub-letting	18	01	16-18
	surveys	07	01	2-7
	tenancy arrangements	15	03	166-173
	terminology of	01	03	86-89
	Wales	07	05	154-160
Manx National Library and Archives		22	02	74-83
maps and plans	see also *agricultural history; archive sources; cartography; estate management; estate records; industrial history; Ordnance Survey; rural settlement; urban history*			
	auction catalogues	13	03	131-139
	bibliography	07	06	196-208
		08	02	61-71
		08	05	167-179
	boundary evidence	15	01	34-40
		15	08	483-485
	Boundary Remark Books	15	01	34-40
	building plans	19	01	3-7
	canals and navigations	08	02	61-71
	charts 17th and 18th c	08	03	86-97
	coal-mining	08	08	275-281
		18	01	5-12
	county maps	08	05	167-179
	deposited plans	04	07	267-274
		07	06	196-208
	early industrial sites	09	02	85-88
	enclosure	07	08	265-274
	estate maps	03	03	115-120
		05	03	66-71
		07	07	223-231
		12	01	26-30
		26	02	66-79

INDEX OF SUBJECTS

subject	sub-heading	vol	no	pages
maps and plans *(cont.)*	estate maps (Scotland)	12	01	26-30
	field boundaries	03	07	292-298
	fire insurance plans	11	06	343-349
	footpaths	01	03	73-77
	general history	01	12	357-360
	house histories	07	06	182-189
	marine charts	08	03	86-97
	military encampments	29	04	212-222
	open field evidence	04	02	73-77
	Ordnance Survey	03	04	170-174
		05	05	130-140
		05	06	166-172
		05	07	202-211
		05	08	251-259
		07	07	223-231
		15	01	34-40
		15	08	483-485
		16	05	282-283
	parish boundaries	18	02	58-64
	railways	08	02	61-71
	Rain's Sunderland	17	07	417-422
	reliability of	08	05	167-179
	roads and highways	08	02	61-71
	Scotland	12	06	296-303
	Sherborne Castle	25	04	231-241
	surveying in 18th c	23	04	218-227
	tithe maps	03	07	292-298
		14	05	262-269
	topographical studies	03	03	115-120
	towns	07	06	196-208
	Tudor charts	08	03	86-97
	VCH use of	22	03	114-127
	Wales	07	05	154-160
maritime history	see also *ports and harbours; ships and shipping*			
		02	07	207-211
	bibliography (charts)	08	03	86-97
	Biscoe, John (explorer)	08	05	160-166
	marine charts	08	03	86-97
	medieval Bristol	20	01	3-15
	Muslim merchant seamen	27	04	225-244
	naval families	07	04	112-118
	naval records	01	11	325-330
	seaports	05	06	177-182
	taxation 18th c	28	02	66-77
markets	see also *commerce and trade; fairs; retailing; urban history*			
	bibliography	08	06	196-204
	development of	11	05	263-277
	early modern	08	04	118-125
	failure (1550-1770)	08	04	118-125
	influence of	21	02	76-78
	manorial development of	29	04	194-211
	newspaper evidence	08	06	196-204

INDEX OF SUBJECTS

subject	sub-heading	vol	no	pages
markets *(cont.)*	place-name evidence	08	06	196-204
	prices of goods	16	08	467-477
	specialisation	08	04	118-125
	street-names	16	04	195-203
	urban growth	08	04	118-125
		08	06	196-204
	urban sources	29	03	167-182
marriage	bigamy	24	03	139-144
	church courts	25	01	7-16
	patterns in 19th c	29	04	223-230
marriage licences		10	06	282-290
masons	see *stonemasons*			
May Day	celebrations	04	07	296-299
mechanics' institutes		07	02	63-65
medals		06	01	2-7
Medieval Archaeology		04	02	65-66
medieval history	bibliography	16	05	260-265
meeting rooms	Polbathic (Cornwall)	16	05	supp
mellgrass		28	04	242-244
memoranda rolls		05	08	242-246
memorials and monuments see also *church (grave) yards; sculpture and carving; stonemasons*				
		01	05	159-162
		04	05	198-201
		06	07	229-233
	battle of Stamford Bridge	04	02	84-85
	brasses on	01	05	159-162
	cemeteries 19th c	28	03	130-144
	church brasses	10	07	339-343
	early carved	04	04	140-142
	Early English	04	05	198-201
	gravestones	13	03	149-159
		14	03	164-167
	heraldry	02	12	362-365
	inscriptions	02	10	297-303
	Leyland (Lancs)	05	04	107-110
	military	07	04	112-118
	Roman	02	10	289-292
	slate headstones	08	06	213-217
	war memorials	20	03	123-125
		26	04	209-222
	Warwick, earls of	03	05	217-219
merchant	meaning of	04	06	227-231
merchant marks		05	04	98-106
Methodism	see also *archive sources; nonconformity; religious history*			
	archives of	03	04	143-149
	chapel accounts	15	01	41-43
	chapels	10	05	253-258
	non-parochial registers	10	02	59-64
	religious census 1851	27	04	194-217
methodology	see *computing; databases; local history; palaeography; research techniques*			
Metropolitan Commons Act 1866		07	07	232-240
microform	archives and books	04	04	162-164

subject	sub-heading	vol	no	pages
midwives		23	03	163-169
	bishops' licences	05	01	2-6
migration	see also *family and kinship; population and demography; population mobility*			
	agricultural labourers	14	01	35-43
	apprenticeships	08	07	232-236
	assimilation of migrants	26	04	223-236
	black history	20	02	59-64
	census evidence	05	08	260-269
		10	05	259-264
		12	02	93-101
		15	01	25-32
		16	08	451-456
		18	02	69-75
	cultural attributes	26	04	223-236
	deposition evidence	17	05	269-276
	family stability	15	30	132-134
	freemen's rolls	09	02	89-95
	from Highlands	18	03	127-135
	general review	03	05	185-189
	Indians in Leicester	28	04	225-241
	industrial areas	18	03	119-126
	intra-urban	21	03	109-119
	Irish in 19th c	29	02	66-75
	Jews to Glasgow	27	02	106-117
	Muslims to North East England	27	04	225-244
	Poor Law records	17	01	19-29
	Sheffield 19th century	29	04	223-230
	Scotland	14	01	35-43
		17	01	19-29
	social structure and	14	05	276-281
		29	04	223-230
	St Helena	28	02	108-122
	surname evidence	13	02	80-86
		14	01	35-43
		16	06	343-345
		16	07	392-404
		20	02	65-72
	Wales to Teesside	12	02	74-79
	Wales to Yorkshire	26	04	223-236
military history	see also *war*			
	archive sources	01	07	205-208
	auxiliary forces	13	08	475-481
	battlefields	01	12	371-374
		04	02	84-85
	bibliography	01	04	102-106
		16	07	405-411
	cannon	17	04	236-241
	castles	04	02	62-64
		04	03	95-97
	Civil War	01	01	13-17
		02	09	261-264

INDEX OF SUBJECTS

subject	sub-heading	vol	no	pages
military history *(cont.)*	Civil War *(cont.)*	26	04	194-208
	Civil War, East Midlands	22	04	191-202
	Civil War, North West Kent	22	03	138-143
	coinage	06	01	2-7
	heraldry	02	08	235-237
	imperialism	22	02	84-88
	lieutenancy and militia	26	03	130-141
	local arms	26	03	130-141
	local history and	07	04	112-118
	Luddite activity	28	01	24-35
	militia 19th c	13	08	475-481
	militia in Civil War	22	04	191-202
	militia rates	26	03	130-141
	militia, Elizabethan	26	03	130-141
	museums	14	02	76-78
	officers' records	06	06	192-197
	pub names	12	01	31-35
	recruitment WW1	17	04	243
	regimental records	04	04	143-152
	St Helena	28	02	108-122
	soldiers' experiences	02	09	261-264
	summer encampments 1778-1782	29	04	212-222
	tournaments	04	02	78-80
	war memorials	26	04	209-222
militia	accounts	01	11	335-338
	administration of	26	04	194-208
	Civil War and	22	04	191-202
	Elizabethan	26	03	130-141
	in 19th c	13	08	475-481
	rates	26	03	130-141
milling industry		07	06	192-195
mills	building plans	19	01	3-7
	Domesday evidence	01	10	297-300
	industrial archaeology	09	04	183-189
	inventory evidence	04	05	186-195
	terminology	02	06	175
	water-powered	02	06	172-174
		15	05	277-287
	woollen	15	05	277-287
minister's accounts		01	04	112-117
moated sites		05	02	34-38
		10	03	135-138
		11	02	89-93
Modern Records Centre, Warwick		12	08	394-400
monasteries	see also *religious history*			
	Chancery proceedings	06	08	254-259
	medieval Bristol	28	01	3-15
	monks and nuns	09	04	175-177
	mortmain, statute of	09	08	387-394
	plans of	01	06	187-191
	pre-Conquest charters	27	01	18-29
	trading activities	05	08	242-246

subject	sub-heading	vol	no	pages
monasteries *(cont.)*	wool trade	04	04	134-139
monasticism	bibliographies	01	04	102-106
Monmouth Rebellion		05	05	141-144
Monumental Brass Society		01	05	159-162
Mortmain, Statute of		09	08	387-394
mosques		28	04	225-241
motor vehicle licenses		17	06	351-357
Municipal Corporations Act 1835		02	06	181
museums		01	07	202-205
	educational role	04	06	242-244
	English Rural Life	03	05	197-207
	folk	03	05	197-207
	heritage industry	24	04	225-228
	Ironbridge	09	06	289-93
	local	01	06	202-204
		04	05	202-205
	military	14	02	76-78
	religious	05	02	51-55
music	bibliography	11	06	315-320
	church bands	06	02	48-54
	folk song	04	05	185
		05	05	141-144
		09	07	343-347
		12	01	13-17
	hymns and psalms	06	02	48-54
	instruments in inventories	04	04	157-161
	local history and	11	06	315-320
	music hall	09	08	379-386
	organs	14	08	482-488
	pleasure gardens	03	08	319-324
	social events	27	03	144-162
music hall	Lancashire cotton towns	09	08	379-386
musters (militia)		26	03	130-141
myths and legends		03	01	1-8
		03	01	9-12
		06	04	134-135
		15	08	492-494
	early genealogies	02	02	37-40
	folk memories	09	06	300-303
	heritage and	26	02	80-88
	Ned Ludd	28	01	24-35
	subterranean passages	02	02	33-36
National Coal Board		08	08	272-281
National Inventory of War Memorials		20	03	123-125
National Library of Scotland		11	08	445-448
National Register of Archives		01	04	127-129
National Register of Archives (Scotland)		01	12	374-377
		17	01	11-18
National Secular Society		08	06	221-227
National Trust	controversies involving	26	02	80-88
	Scotland	25	04	223-230
	social/political composition	26	02	80-88

subject	sub-heading	vol	no	pages
nationalism	Scottish	25	04	223-230
new towns	Victorian	10	04	186-195
Newcomen Society		04	06	245-250
newspapers		02	04	97-101
	advertisements	09	07	334-337
		10	06	271-276
		14	03	134-141
	farm sale advertisements	28	01	36-49
	history	16	08	479-482
	holiday resorts	13	06	323-331
	housing information	12	07	353-359
	indexing projects	05	07	212-217
		14	03	143-148
	London Gazette	15	04	212-217
	retailing evidence	29	03	167-182
	trade union	13	05	259-262
	urban history	11	06	321-326
	poverty reported	08	03	98-106
nonconformity	see also *churches; Methodism; puritans; religious history*			
	cemeteries 19th c	28	03	130-144
	chapels	10	05	253-258
	Chartism and	03	01	13-19
	Christian (Plymouth) Brethren	14	08	478-481
	Congregationalism	03	05	208-212
	Dr Williams's Library	09	03	115-120
	early modern	07	08	253-257
	licensing of meeting places	05	01	2-6
	Methodist archives	03	04	143-149
	non-parochial registers	10	02	59-64
	oaths concerning	02	11	337-338
	religious census 1851	11	07	375-381
		27	04	194-217
	religious returns 1829	17	08	483-489
		18	04	162-167
	religious tracts	10	03	116-124
	sources	08	04	131-134
	temperance movement	08	05	180-186
	under-registration	06	06	198-203
numismatics		02	01	1-3
		06	01	2-7
		07	03	88-91
	Anglo-Saxon	25	01	3-6
	trade tokens	06	02	55-61
nurse-children		19	03	100-106
oaths	registration of	02	11	337-338
occupations and employment	see also *agricultural history; agricultural labourers; commerce and trade; industrial history; industries; trades and crafts*			
	agricultural workers	03	02	49-54
		13	06	353-359
		15	01	25-32
		26	01	16-35
		27	03	130-143

INDEX OF SUBJECTS

subject	sub-heading	vol	no	pages
occupations and employment *(cont.)*	agricultural workers *(cont.)*	29	02	66-75
	apprenticeships	02	12	357-361
		08	07	232-236
		09	02	89-95
		12	03-04	139-145
		14	01	11-17
		14	07	400-406
		17	05	269-276
		19	02	51-55
		25	04	194-208
	Black Country	18	03	119-126
	book trade	26	04	237-245
	census analysis	12	02	93-101
	census data	05	08	260-269
		11	02	85-88
		16	08	451-456
		17	04	199-204
		27	03	130-143
	census definitions	13	08	481-487
	census reliability	23	04	205-216
	coal-mining	18	01	5-12
		26	04	223-236
	computer analysis	18	02	69-75
	craft apprenticeships	14	07	400-406
	databases	16	05	266-277
	directory evidence	11	02	85-88
		17	06	343-350
	doctors	04	08	320-324
	Dorset inventories	12	05	228-234
	dual occupations	11	04	200-206
	early car owners	17	06	351-357
	freemen's rolls	09	02	89-95
	friendly society members	24	04	229-242
	hidden economy	17	04	226-235
	holiday resorts	13	06	323-331
	Indians in Leicester	28	04	225-241
	industrial structure	12	03-04	152-156
	Irish community	29	02	66-75
	Jews in Glasgow	27	02	106-117
	licensed trade	25	01	31-42
	marriage licence evidence	10	06	282-290
	mass unemployment	27	03	163-182
	medieval borough	02	11	321-325
	metal trades Sheffield 19th c	29	04	223-230
	migration 19th c	12	02	74-79
	Muslim merchant seamen	27	04	225-244
	occupational structures	11	06	340-343
	open and closed villages	06	08	271-278
	parish register evidence	15	06	361
		11	06	340-343
	paupers	20	01	9-19
	penny capitalism	17	04	226-235

INDEX OF SUBJECTS

subject	sub-heading	vol	no	pages
occupations and employment *(cont.)*	police	18	03	127-135
	probate inventories	04	06	227-231
		12	05	228-234
	professions	04	08	320-324
	railway workers	11	01	30-34
	rural communities	06	08	271-278
		18	02	69-75
	rural trades and crafts	28	03	145-158
	rural Wales 19th c	09	04	178-183
	seasonal work	09	04	178-183
	servants	02	11	334-336
	Sheffield metal trades in 19th c	29	04	223-230
	sources 20th c	20	03	109-117
	stonemasons	02	08	232-234
		21	02	60-65
	straw-plaiting	19	03	107-113
	surnames and	10	04	171-177
		27	04	i-xx
	teaching profession	12	03-04	161-166
	timber crafts	20	02	73-79
	trade tokens	06	02	55-61
	unofficial	17	04	226-235
	urban 17th c	20	03	128-136
	Victorian Whitby	28	02	78-93
	wartime agriculture	29	02	76-90
	women	29	02	66-75
	women in agriculture	27	03	130-143
	women traders 18th c	17	03	158-162
	workhouse masters	16	02	93-100
oral history	agricultural labourer	09	07	338-342
	anecdotal	05	05	141-144
	approaches to	10	04	183-185
	bibliography	14	04	211-221
		15	07	414-431
	black communities	20	02	59-64
	community projects	13	05	276-280
	dangers inherent in	10	07	334-339
	early 20th c	20	03	109-117
	elderly people	03	04	150-152
	ethnic communities	19	01	8-15
	folk memories	09	06	300-303
	folk songs	04	05	185
	general review	13	07	408-416
	legends	06	04	134-135
	local history and	22	01	14-7
	post-war families	28	04	i-xvi
	publishing	27	04	218-224
	recent work (1976)	12	03-04	131-135
	suburban areas	11	05	285-289
	Swansea project 1975-78	14	05	284-288
	techniques	13	07	408-416
Ordnance Survey	see also *maps and plans*			

subject	sub-heading	vol	no	pages
Ordnance Survey *(cont.)*		01	12	357-360
		05	05	130-140
		07	07	223-231
	administrative maps	05	08	251-259
	archaeological sites	03	04	170-174
	boundaries on maps	15	08	483-485
	Boundary Remark Books	15	01	34-40
	county maps and	08	05	167-179
	field books	16	05	282-283
	historical maps	05	06	166-172
	large scale maps	05	07	202-211
	parish boundaries	15	01	34-40
	small-scale maps	05	08	251-259
	town plans	05	08	251-259
overseers of the poor		06	04	110-114
	accounts	01	09	269-272
		20	01	9-19
	case study	16	01	15-20
	status/position of	25	03	164-177
owners of land	1873 returns	02	08	230-231
Oxford English Dictionary		24	03	164-173
Oxfordshire Local History Association		14	03	131-133
pacifism	wartime labourers	29	02	76-90
palaeography		01	05	146-154
palaeography	analysing handwriting	26	02	89-101
	bibliography	16	06	327-334
	medieval	03	02	81-94
		07	03	88-91
	transcribing registers	07	05	138-145
	Tudor document	22	01	41-42
pamphlets		05	05	141-144
		14	07	419-427
	broadsheets	25	02	66-76
	Fawcett Library	23	02	92-97
paper-making		08	02	42-46
pargetting		01	12	365-367
parish and township administration see also *counties; courts; local government; manorial system*				
		05	04	111-114
	apprenticeships	02	12	357-361
		14	07	400-406
	boundaries	15	08	483-485
		18	02	58-64
		27	01	3-17
	briefs	02	06	165-167
	census returns	14	02	79-90
	church records	02	03	82-86
	churchwardens	01	08	234-237
		06	04	110-114
	constables	01	02	38-42
		01	11	335-338
		04	08	325-328
		06	04	110-114

subject	sub-heading	vol	no	pages
parish and township administration *(cont.)*	detached portions	18	02	58-64
	evolution of structure	27	01	3-17
	fieldmasters	06	04	110-114
	glossary	27	01	3-17
	highway surveyors	01	10	301-304
		06	04	110-114
	inventories of church goods	07	07	219-222
	kirk session registers	11	04	229-233
	legislative structure	27	01	3-17
	local taxes and rates	12	01	7-12
	manorial involvement	27	01	3-17
	Middlesex	23	03	155-162
	minor subdivisions	15	08	483-485
	overseers of the poor	01	09	269-272
		06	04	110-114
		16	01	15-20
		25	03	164-177
		27	01	3-17
	parish clerks (medieval)	03	05	213-216
	parish records	02	03	69-71
		06	04	110-114
	parish registers	01	07	198-202
		04	06	232-234
		06	05	146-151
		06	06	198-203
	parish system	21	01	4-10
	Poor Law	02	09	268-270
		20	01	9-19
		27	01	3-17
	Poor Law, Old	12	03-04	136-139
		14	01	11-17
	poor relief	25	03	164-177
	proto-industrial society	27	02	78-90
	regional variation	27	01	3-17
	removal orders	05	04	111-114
	roads and highways	27	01	3-17
	sanitary provision	21	04	156-161
	terminology	01	04	122-124
	terriers	01	12	361-364
	tithes	01	12	361-364
	tithings	27	01	3-17
	vagrancy	02	10	309-310
	vestries	01	08	234-237
	water supplies	26	03	155-167
	workhouses	10	02	70-75
parish boundaries	Boundary Remark Books	15	01	34-40
parish chests		02	03	69-71
parish clerks	bishops' licences	05	01	2-6
	medieval	03	05	213-216
parish councils		17	04	212-218
	councillors	19	04	159-161
parish histories		18	01	23

subject	sub-heading	vol	no	pages
parish histories *(cont.)*	publishing	04	03	110-115
parish magazines		16	08	457-466
parish records		01	08	234-237
		02	03	69-71
		06	04	110-114
	civil war evidence	22	03	138-143
	coal-mining evidence	18	01	5-12
	enclosure maps/awards	07	08	265-274
	highway surveyors	01	10	301-304
	study packs	18	01	23
	terminology	01	04	122-124
	Wales	07	05	154-160
parish registers		01	06	198-201
		01	07	198-202
		04	06	232-234
	burial statistics	23	04	199-204
	Catholic registration	15	05	288-295
	census data 1831	14	02	79-90
	defects of	06	06	198-203
	genealogy	07	06	178-181
	kinship evidence	26	01	36-47
	nurse children in	19	03	100-106
	occupation evidence	11	06	340-343
		15	06	361
	plague mortality	14	06	332-340
	population history	06	05	146-150
		06	06	198-203
		14	05	276-281
	record linkages	27	02	78-90
	regional variability	18	03	136-141
	reliability of	14	05	276-281
	social structure	14	05	276-281
	surname evidence	17	07	391-395
	transcribing rules	07	05	138-145
	transcripts	22	02	68-73
	Yorkshire Archaeological Society	19	04	170-173
parishes	ecclesiastical	21	01	4-10
parks		03	08	332-349
	auction catalogues	13	03	131-139
	Bridgeman, Charles	06	03	91-96
	deer parks	26	02	66-79
	inventory of Kip engravings	04	01	23-25
	landscaping	25	04	231-241
	relict hedgerows	18	02	65-68
	Repton, Humphrey	03	08	332-349
	Victorian development	20	04	158-165
	village destruction	28	04	208-216
	Weston-super-Mare	20	04	158-165
parliament		02	03	65-68
	acts of	04	06	219-226
		04	07	267-274
	constituencies 1867	13	07	416-424

subject	sub-heading	vol	no	pages
parliament *(cont.)*	deposited plans	04	07	267-274
		07	06	196-208
	enclosure legislation	29	01	25-42
	private bills	04	07	267-274
	records of	04	06	219-226
		04	08	307-314
		04	08	354-358
	women voters 1918-1945	28	03	159-175
parliamentary papers		04	08	307-314
	coal industry	08	08	272-281
	rural settlement	07	01	7-13
	workhouses	10	02	70-75
Patent Office	records of	09	06	275-279
patent rolls		01	02	47-51
		02	11	321-325
patents	as source	09	06	275-279
pawnbroking		20	01	24-30
peasant revolts	France	11	04	188-199
peasantry	definitions of	11	04	200-206
	education	11	04	188-199
penny capitalism		17	04	226-235
petty sessions		15	02	74-79
pewter	probate inventories	17	02	85-100
photographers	Bale, Stewart	18	04	190-191
	Barber, James	18	02	80-81
	Bustin family	20	04	187-189
	Cleet, James Henry	19	04	174-176
	Flagg, Amy	19	04	170-173
	Harrison, William Jerome	20	04	166-172
	Hedderley, James	18	03	142-144
	Hill, William	19	02	74-76
	Thurston, Frederick	19	01	27-29
	Warham, Thomas	20	01	37-39
	Wilson, George Washington	19	03	124-126
photographs		01	10	293-296
		05	05	151-154
	Ancient Order of Foresters	16	03	169
	Aquitainia at Liverpool	16	04	234
	as historical source	15	08	468-473
	boot repair shop	16	02	101
	cataloguing methods	13	01	22-36
	child prisoners	15	06	366
	clipping the church	14	08	489
	colliery strike	16	05	298
	congregation St Mary, Nottingham	17	01	45
	floating church	16	07	431
	Frith collection	18	01	24
	historical evidence	02	02	41-43
		13	01	22-36
	hustings 1868 election	14	06	359
	Ipswich Ragged School	14	01	34
	Lincoln typhoid epidemic	14	03	142

subject	sub-heading	vol	no	pages
photographs *(cont.)*	night-soil men	15	05	300
	New York trolley conductorettes	16	01	55
	open air baptism	15	02	94
	Pax public house	16	08	489
	rag-well	15	03	166-173
	railway accident	15	01	44
	recruitment WW1	17	04	243
	reliability of	15	08	468-473
	Scotland	12	06	296-303
	seaside resorts	17	02	113
	Shrovetide football	14	05	292
	unsorted documents	15	04	229
	Wolverton railway works	17	03	169
photography	aerial	05	04	115-120
		15	07	402-405
		16	08	483-488
	cities in 19th c	09	08	400-406
	documents	05	03	77-79
	historical use of	20	04	166-72
	surveys	09	05	222-225
pictures and illustrations		05	05	151-154
		06	03	74-78
		07	02	59-62
	cities in 19th c	09	08	400-406
	medieval Bristol	28	01	3-15
	photography	02	02	41-43
	Scottish National Portrait Gallery	11	07	382-384
	sources	07	02	59-62
		10	07	355-360
	town engravings	10	03	139-141
	valentine cards	09	03	134-141
place-names		02	02	44-47
	Anglo-Saxon	22	03	114-127
	bibliography	17	07	396-404
	bridges and fords	07	08	250-252
	Celtic	22	03	114-127
	charter evidence	13	04	209-216
	charters	01	08	241-245
	chronology	11	01	3-7
	deer parks	26	02	66-79
	dumble [rushes]	11	02	63-67
	East Anglia and Canada	04	01	9-11
	elements in	01	02	55-59
	estate maps	07	07	223-231
	feet of fines	24	02	66-82
	field-names	13	07	388-396
		17	05	285-289
	glossary of elements	22	03	114-127
	imperialism and	22	02	84-88
	industrial history	07	05	146-149
		08	01	16-21
	Latin-derived	22	03	114-127

INDEX OF SUBJECTS

subject	sub-heading	vol	no	pages
place-names *(cont.)*	local history and	01	02	51-55
	locative surnames	27	04	i-xx
	markets and fairs	08	06	196-204
	medieval agriculture	26	02	66-79
	meols	28	04	242-244
	methodology	02	02	44-48
		22	03	114-127
	mills and milling	07	06	192-195
	misidentification	13	04	209-216
	modern industrial	08	01	16-21
	origins of	01	02	51-55
	pre-Conquest	01	11	340-343
	primary towns	11	05	263-277
	pub names	12	01	31-35
	recent work (1974)	11	01	3-7
	review (1992)	22	03	114-127
	routeways	12	05	212-220
	salt industry	07	05	146-149
	Scandinavian	22	03	114-127
	street-names	01	09	278-282
		08	08	288-291
		16	04	195-203
	surnames	10	01	3-7
		10	04	171-177
		10	05	227-233
	topographical	12	06	273-277
	towns	10	06	302-304
	Wales	25	03	178-185
	woodland evidence	16	02	73-82
plague		05	03	85-89
		14	06	332-340
plea rolls		01	05	155-158
poetry and verse	valentine cards	09	03	134-141
police		14	04	226-232
	archives	02	04	111-113
	birthplaces of	18	03	127-135
	crime studies	14	08	454-459
	General Strike	16	01	36-48
		16	02	83-89
	local 19th c	14	08	454-459
	migration to Glasgow	18	03	127-135
politics, local	agricultural unions	13	06	353-359
	Bexley (Kent)	11	05	285-289
	Chartist movement	03	01	11-19
	clergy influence	15	07	388-401
	co-operative movement	09	04	163-171
	constituencies 1867	13	07	416-424
	county councils	23	01	31-39
	elections 1860s	13	07	416-424
	enclosure legislation	29	01	25-42
	fascism	27	02	106-117
	garden cities movement	27	01	30-47

subject	sub-heading	vol	no	pages
politics, local *(cont.)*	General Strike	16	01	36-48
	health reform	21	04	168-176
	Hertfordshire	23	01	31-39
	in 17th century	26	04	194-208
	influential personalities	15	07	388-401
	local affiliations	23	02	103-110
	mechanics' institutes	07	02	63-65
	parish councils	17	04	212-218
	political parties	02	03	65-68
		20	03	109-17
		23	02	103-110
	Radicalism early 19th c	25	01	17-30
	relationship to philanthropy	27	03	144-162
	rural labour movements	03	02	49-54
	school boards	09	03	130-134
	secularism	08	06	221-227
	street-names	22	02	84-88
	suffrage movement	11	02	77-79
	temperance movement	08	05	180-186
	West Ham	20	03	109-117
	women's allegiances 1918-45	28	03	159-175
	women's history	23	02	92-97
poll tax		03	07	271-278
pollution	lead-smelting	24	03	130-138
	rural sanitation	21	04	156-161
poor	charitable bequests	15	04	225-226
	eligibility for relief	15	06	358-360
	medical provision for	10	05	221-226
	welfare of	08	03	98-106
Poor Laws	see also *local government; poor; poverty and paupers; social history*			
	accounts	01	09	269-272
	administration (18th c)	28	02	66-77
	Amendment Act 1834	02	01	11-15
	apprenticeship	14	01	11-17
		14	07	400-406
		19	02	51-55
	bibliography	12	05	206-211
	bigamy among poor	24	03	139-144
	Bristol 1816-1817	25	01	17-30
	case study (Old Poor Law)	16	01	15-20
	charitable bequests	15	04	225-226
	computer project	11	08	452-456
	eligibility for relief	15	06	358-360
	Guardians	16	01	25-31
		16	02	93-100
	Hanwell (Middlesex)	25	03	164-177
	industrialising areas	27	02	78-90
	local impact (New)	12	05	206-211
	non able-bodied poor	20	01	9-19
	out-relief	16	01	25-31
	overseers	06	04	110-114
	overseers' records	14	01	11-17

INDEX OF SUBJECTS

subject	sub-heading	vol	no	pages
Poor Laws *(cont.)*	parish workhouses	10	02	70-75
	parochial administration	27	01	3-17
	politics of	12	05	206-211
	population mobility and	17	01	19-29
	rating records	28	02	66-77
	records (general)	12	03-04	136-139
	removal orders	05	04	111-114
	recent research (1977)	12	05	206-211
	rural unrest and	03	02	49-54
	scandals, Victorian	16	02	93-100
	Scotland	17	01	19-29
	self-help and	24	04	229-242
	settlement criteria	02	09	268-270
	settlement procedures	12	03-04	136-139
	Shropshire	14	01	11-17
	sick and infirm	20	01	9-19
	Speenhamland period	12	05	206-211
	Union archives	02	01	11-15
	vagrancy	02	10	309-311
		21	02	66-69
	workhouse inmates	11	08	452-456
	workhouse staff	16	02	93-100
population and demography	see also *census data; census returns; censuses; family and kinship; population mobility; rural settlement; urban history*			
	bibliography	10	06	291-294
		16	04	207-212
	birth rates	09	01	27-35
	burial statistics	23	04	199-204
	census analyses	08	01	2-10
		10	05	259-264
		12	02	93-101
		15	01	25-32
		16	05	266-277
		16	08	451-456
		18	02	69-75
		22	04	184-190
		29	04	223-230
	census enumerators	18	01	19-20
	census reliability	23	04	205-216
	census returns	01	06	174-177
		05	08	260-269
		06	05	146-150
		10	01	13-26
		11	03	155-161
		14	02	79-90
		29	04	223-230
	changes 1780-1850	14	05	276-281
	civil registration	03	03	108-112
	computer analysis	15	08	464-467
		16	60	335-342
	electoral registers	11	01	30-34
	emigration	04	01	9-11

subject	sub-heading	vol	no	pages
population and demography *(cont.)*	family reconstitution	06	05	146-150
		06	06	198-203
		09	01	9-15
		25	04	209-222
		27	02	78-90
	family stability	15	03	132-134
		29	04	223-230
	fertility	06	05	146-150
	hearth tax	11	07	385-389
	house repopulation	13	02	86-97
		14	03	134-141
	hundred rolls	05	01	9-16
	immigration in cities	28	04	225-241
	intra-urban mobility	21	03	109-119
	Irish migration	29	02	66-75
	Jewish migrations	27	02	106-117
	lay subsidy evidence	04	03	101-109
	local history and micro-studies	06	02	38-44
		18	03	119-126
	migration	03	05	185-189
		04	01	9-11
		12	02	74-79
		18	03	127-135
		26	40	223-236
		27	02	106-117
		29	02	66-75
		29	04	223-230
	mortality crises	06	05	146-150
		06	06	198-203
	mortality rates	09	01	27-35
	nurse children	19	03	100-106
	overcrowding	10	05	259-264
		16	03	156-160
		18	03	106-111
		29	02	66-75
	parish register statistics 1831	14	02	79-90
	parish registers	06	05	146-150
		06	06	198-203
		07	05	138-145
	parliamentary records	04	08	307-314
	plague mortality	14	06	332-340
	poll tax records	03	07	271-278
	protestation returns	14	03	134-141
	record linkages	27	02	78-90
	rural mortality	16	01	21-23
	rural Scotland	15	08	456-463
	social structures	14	05	276-281
		29	04	223-230
	sources 1500-1760	04	04	129-133
		04	05	182-184
	sources 17th c	14	03	134-141
	statistical analysis 19th c	09	01	27-35

subject	sub-heading	vol	no	pages
population and demography *(cont.)*	surname evidence	08	08	299-302
		16	07	392-404
		27	04	i-xx
	urban 17th c	20	03	128-136
	urban 18th c	10	01	13-26
		10	03	142-146
	urban mortality	21	04	168-176
	Welsh sources	10	06	291-294
population mobility	see also *census data; census returns; migration; population and demography*			
	black history	20	02	59-64
	business records	24	01	4-14
	census analysis	05	08	260-269
		15	01	25-32
		16	05	266-277
		16	08	451-456
		17	04	199-204
		18	02	69-75
		29	04	223-230
	deposition books	17	05	269-276
	family stability	15	03	132-134
	freemen's rolls	09	02	89-95
	industrialisation	18	03	119-126
		29	04	223-230
	intra-urban migration	21	03	109-119
	medieval surnames	13	02	80-86
	migration to NE England	27	04	225-244
	movement from Highlands	18	03	127-135
	nurse children	19	03	100-106
	Poor Law records	17	01	19-29
	surname evidence	08	08	299-302
		16	06	343-345
		17	07	391-395
		20	02	65-72
		27	04	i-xx
	vagrancy	21	02	66-69
ports and harbours		02	07	207-211
	19th century	05	06	177-182
	conference report	14	05	270-275
	medieval Bristol	28	01	3-15
	medieval trade	22	01	18-40
	research topics	07	03	84-87
Post Office	mailcoaches	14	06	341-346
	telegraph system	24	03	153-163
postal services	Berkshire 18th c	29	03	152-166
	mailcoaches	14	06	341-346
pottery	prehistoric	01	12	378-381
	Roman and medieval	02	06	161-164
pottery industry		08	02	54-60
		08	03	78-85
	Rockingham	24	01	37-43
poverty and paupers	see also *poor; Poor Laws*			
	apprenticeships	02	12	357-361

subject	sub-heading	vol	no	pages
poverty and paupers (cont.)	apprenticeships (cont.)	19	02	51-55
	attitudes to poor	12	05	206-211
	bigamy among poor	24	03	139-44
	case study	16	01	15-20
	charitable relief	15	04	225-226
		27	03	144-162
	crime and	15	02	74-79
	definitions of	15	06	358-360
	enumeration of paupers	25	01	17-30
	experimental solutions	25	01	17-30
	extent	25	01	17-30
	geographical concentration	16	01	25-31
		21	03	109-119
	lay subsidy evidence	04	03	101-109
	Liverpool 19th c	08	03	98-106
	medical provision	10	05	221-226
	pawning	20	01	24-30
	relief	14	01	11-17
		15	06	358-360
		25	01	17-30
		25	03	164-177
	removal orders	05	04	111-114
	self-help	24	04	229-242
	social deprivation	15	02	74-79
	urban 17th c	20	03	128-136
	urban 20th c	20	03	109-117
	urban poor	21	03	109-119
	vagrancy	02	10	309-310
		21	02	66-69
presbyterianism	sources	08	04	131-134
prices	farm produce 19th c	13	05	270-276
	honey	29	03	130-151
	inventory valuations	16	08	467-477
		17	02	85-100
	livestock in inventories	17	02	85-100
	medieval	02	09	271-272
	past equivalents	02	08	235-244
	post-Reformation listings	02	10	304-208
	postal services 18th c	29	03	152-166
	probate inventories	17	02	85-100
	probate valuations	16	08	467-477
		17	02	85-100
	rural living standards	03	02	49-54
	timber industry	20	02	73-79
priest holes		06	08	266-269
printing industry		03	07	299-300
		26	04	237-245
	newspapers and journals	16	08	479-482
probate records		01	09	265-268
		02	03	76-79
		06	03	86-90
	accounts	21	02	51-59

INDEX OF SUBJECTS

subject	sub-heading	vol	no	pages
probate records *(cont.)*	agricultural evidence	04	05	186-195
		16	03	133-145
	appraisers of inventories	16	03	133-145
	architecture, evidence for	12	05	235-240
	bigamy, evidence of	24	03	139-144
	books in	11	01	14-17
		15	08	478-482
	charitable bequests	16	01	21-23
	church courts	04	01	12-22
		25	01	7-16
	commissary court testaments	17	01	4-10
	computer analysis	11	03	129-133
		26	02	89-101
	dialect and terminology	24	03	164-173
	disputed wills	04	01	12-22
	employment evidence	12	05	228-234
	estate values	16	08	467-477
	farmers' inventories	12	05	228-234
	genealogy	07	06	178-181
	handwriting analyses	26	02	89-101
	housing, evidence for	04	04	157-161
		16	03	133-145
	industrial evidence	16	03	133-145
	legal procedures	12	01	36-37
		16	03	133-145
		16	04	217-227
	literacy evidence	16	03	133-145
		21	01	16-19
	livestock valuations	17	02	85-100
	merchants	04	06	227-231
	money-lending evidence	12	05	228-234
		28	04	228-234
	PCC	14	04	222-225
	pewter and brass	17	02	85-100
	printed indexes post-1858	15	04	218-220
	probate inventories	04	05	186-195
		04	06	227-231
		04	08	320-324
		12	01	36-37
		12	05	228-234
		12	05	235-240
		14	04	222-225
		16	03	133-145
		16	04	217-227
		16	08	467-477
		17	02	85-100
		20	03	128-136
	probate valuations	11	02	68-71
	professional people	04	08	320-324
	puritanism	16	04	213-216
	record linkages	27	02	78-90
	Scotland	17	01	4-10

subject	sub-heading	vol	no	pages
probate records *(cont.)*	social structure and	28	04	194-207
	urban 17th c	20	03	128-136
	valuations	11	02	68-71
		16	08	467-477
		17	02	85-100
	Wales	07	05	154-160
		25	03	178-183
	wealth assessments	28	04	194-207
proofs of age		05	07	224-230
protest movements	French peasants	11	04	188-199
Protestation returns		02	08	251
		14	03	134-141
	population evidence	04	05	182-184
public health	see also *disease and illness; health and medical care; hospitals; local government; population and demography*			
	baths	25	03	142-152
	cemeteries 19th c	28	03	130-144
	development of	14	04	202-210
	medical care 18th c	20	04	173-186
	MOH reports	12	07	353-359
	night-soil men	15	05	300
	overcrowding	16	03	156-160
	reform of	21	04	156-161
		21	04	168-176
	rural	23	03	163-169
	sources 19th c	14	04	202-10
	sources 20th c	20	03	109-117
	urban poor	08	03	98-106
	water supplies	26	03	155-167
	Welsh records	14	04	202-210
	women and	23	02	92-97
Public Record Office	see also *archive services*			
		06	02	45-48
	army officers' records	06	06	192-197
	borough records	02	11	321-325
	Chancery records	06	08	254-9
		17	08	475-482
	church history	07	01	17-27
	courts of equity	17	07	408-416
		17	08	475-482
	feet of fines	01	01	5-8
		24	02	66-82
	inquisitions post mortem	06	07	235-242
	inventories of church goods	07	07	219-222
	lay subsidies	03	08	325-328
	maps and plans	07	06	196-208
	memoranda rolls	05	08	242-246
	minister's accounts	01	04	112-117
	non-parochial registers	10	02	59-64
	patent records	09	06	275-279
	plea rolls	01	05	155-158
	poll tax records	03	07	271-278

INDEX OF SUBJECTS

subject	sub-heading	vol	no	pages
Public Record Office	Poor Law records	16	02	93-100
(cont.)	public health records	14	04	202-210
	Welsh records	07	06	189-191
publishing local history		01	10	305-308
		02	01	8-11
		02	04	97-101
		02	05	130-133
	19th century	26	01	3-14
	archive guides	13	07	425-430
		13	08	468-471
	bibliography (1980)	14	04	211-221
	Chepstow	02	07	212-214
	church guides	10	07	344-350
	class projects	22	02	58-67
	computer databases	29	01	43-51
	copyright issues	08	03	106-108
	general survey	12	03-04	131-135
		12	07	343-348
		14	07	419-427
	Hampton-on-Thames	03	05	183-184
	Harrow	10	08	401-403
	Hatfield	05	03	81-84
	indexing techniques	17	05	281-284
	journal title	07	03	78-83
	Lincolnshire history project	09	03	111-114
	local societies	12	06	277-283
	maps and plans	17	03	135-140
	Middlesex VCH	23	03	155-162
	National Trust books	26	02	80-88
	newspaper indexing	05	07	212-217
	Northamptonshire	19	04	167-169
	open air schools	29	02	102-113
	parish histories	04	03	110-115
	parish packs	18	01	23
	practical advice	12	07	360-364
		12	08	421-429
		13	03	160-170
		13	04	224-232
	printers' specimens	03	07	299-300
	QueenSpark Books' experience	27	04	218-224
	railways	05	01	17-22
	self-help	16	02	90-92
	The Common Stream	12	08	391-394
	The Local Historian	22	01	8-13
	town trails parodied	15	05	272-276
puritanism		01	02	59-61
		07	08	253-257
	literacy and	11	01	14-17
	probate evidence	16	04	213-216
Quakers	archives	03	02	55-61
		08	07	258-262
	journals	21	02	70-75

subject	sub-heading	vol	no	pages
quantity surveying		22	01	41-42
quarrying		21	02	60-65
quarter sessions	taxation and rates	12	01	7-12
	trading evidence	08	06	196-204
Queen Anne's Bounty		09	05	215-221
QueenSpark Books		27	04	218-224
quo warranto inquiries		02	11	321-325
rabbits		09	02	59-64
		18	01	13-15
		18	02	53-57
racial conflict	Muslims in NE 1919	27	04	225-244
racial discrimination		19	01	8-15
	anti-Semitism	27	02	106-117
	Leicester	28	04	225-241
Radcliffe estate (Yorkshire)		23	04	188-198
Railway & Canal Historical Society		02	09	257-260
railways	accidents	15	01	44
	archives	04	08	329-334
		12	08	394-400
	bibliography	08	01	10-15
	conference report	14	05	270-275
	consequences of	03	05	191-197
	early coalfield	16	07	418-424
	economic and social impact	03	05	191-197
	GWR workers	11	01	31-3
	maps and plans	08	02	61-71
	research topics	07	03	84-87
	resort development	24	04	206-216
		28	02	78-93
	societies	02	09	257-260
	sources	01	03	90-94
		08	01	10-15
	urban development	10	03	126-134
	Wolverton works	17	03	169
	writing their history	05	01	17-22
		08	01	10-15
rate books		17	05	277-280
	regional variability	18	03	136-141
reading rooms		20	04	155-157
Rebecca Riots		08	07	255-257
record linkages		13	02	86-97
		25	04	209-222
		27	02	78-90
recusancy	see *Catholicism; religious history*			
Reformation	Bristol	28	01	3-15
	local effects	07	08	253-257
regimental records		04	04	143-152
regional history	computing	25	04	209-222
	income variations 1803	13	06	332-338
	local history and	06	01	11-17
		06	02	38-44
		06	04	121-124

INDEX OF SUBJECTS

subject	sub-heading	vol	no	pages
regional history *(cont.)*	local history and *(cont.)*	13	01	1-11
		14	06	325-331
		14	07	392-399
		21	03	99-108
		26	01	36-47
		29	04	256-262
	qualifications	16	07	388-391
regnal years		02	06	176-180
	tables of	01	01	23-26
religious history	see also *Catholicism; churches; clergy; memorials and monuments; nonconformity; Quakers*			
	archaeology	25	01	3-6
	archives	09	05	215-221
	bibliographies	08	07	237-242
		09	02	65-74
		09	06	283-289
		16	03	151-155
		27	04	194-217
	bishops' licences	05	01	2-6
	bishops' returns 1563, 1603	04	04	129-133
		15	03	155-156
	Catholicism	02	11	337-339
		06	08	266-269
		09	06	283-289
		15	03	155-156
		15	05	288-295
		17	08	483-489
		27	04	194-217
	cemeteries 19th c	28	03	130-144
	census 1676	04	05	182-184
	census 1851	11	07	375-381
		27	04	194-217
	Chancery proceedings	06	08	254-259
	chapel accounts	15	01	41-43
	chapels	10	05	253-258
		21	01	4-10
	Christian (Plymouth) Brethren	14	08	478-481
	church (grave) yards	06	07	229-233
		13	03	149-159
		14	03	164-167
		16	07	412-417
		23	02	66-84
	church architecture	02	01	15-18
		07	02	53-59
	church bands	06	02	48-54
	church brasses	10	07	339-343
	church briefs	02	06	165-167
	church buildings	05	04	107-110
		07	01	17-27
	Church Commissioners	09	05	215-221
	church courts	01	09	265-268
		02	02	50-53

subject	sub-heading	vol	no	pages
religious history *(cont.)*	church courts *(cont.)*	04	01	12-22
		07	01	17-27
		21	03	120-125
		25	01	7-16
	church furnishings	05	04	107-110
		07	08	253-257
		22	04	203-207
		23	03	130-145
		27	02	91-105
	church goods	07	07	219-222
	church music	06	02	48-54
		11	06	315-320
	church records	05	02	44-50
	church seating	04	01	12-22
		22	04	203-207
		27	02	91-105
	clergy	01	02	59-61
	clergy charities	11	08	465-469
	clergy inventories	04	08	320-324
	clergy records	02	03	82-86
	clipping the church	14	08	489
	commissary courts	17	01	4-10
	congregation 18th c	17	01	45
	Congregationalism	03	05	208-212
	cricket teams	25	02	95-108
	deposition books	17	05	269-276
	dioceses of 1540s	28	01	3-15
	Dr Williams's Library	09	03	115-120
	early carved stones	04	04	140-142
	early sites	11	05	263-277
	ecclesiastical parishes	27	01	3-17
	education (Scotland)	17	01	11-18
	education in 16th c	11	08	473-476
	electoral issues 1860s	13	07	416-424
	episcopal estates	11	05	263-277
	evangelical tracts	10	03	116-124
	evangelicalism 19th c	15	07	388-401
	fonts	23	03	130-145
	Foster, Canon C.W.	06	05	157-162
	French peasant risings	11	04	188-199
	glebe terriers	12	05	235-240
	glossary (churches)	02	01	15-18
	graffiti evidence	23	01	4-19
	graveyard memorials	23	02	66-84
	heresy	28	01	3-15
	historical sources	07	01	17-27
	iconoclasm	23	03	130-145
	Incorporated Church Building Soc	27	02	91-105
	Indians in Leicester	28	04	225-241
	influence of clergy	15	07	388-401
	interdenominational sports	25	02	95-108
	inventories of church goods	07	07	219-222

subject	sub-heading	vol	no	pages
religious history *(cont.)*	kirk sessions	11	04	229-233
	licensing of meeting houses	05	01	2-6
	liturgy and architecture	07	02	53-59
	medieval Bristol	28	01	3-15
	medieval monuments	04	05	198-201
	medieval parish clerks	03	05	213-216
	Methodism	03	04	143-149
	Methodism 1851	27	04	194-217
	monastic chronicles	02	04	102-105
	monastic trade	04	04	134-139
	monks and nuns	09	04	175-177
	monuments	02	10	297-303
		02	12	362-365
		04	05	198-201
		05	04	107-110
		06	07	229-233
		16	07	412-417
		23	02	66-84
	museums (Europe)	05	02	51-55
	music	06	02	48-54
	non-parochial registers	10	02	59-64
	nonconformity	08	04	131-134
	open air baptism	15	02	94
	parish magazines	16	08	457-466
	parish records	06	04	110-114
	parish registers	01	07	198-202
		04	06	232-234
		06	05	146-150
		06	06	198-203
		07	05	138-145
		07	06	178-181
		11	06	340-343
		14	02	79-90
		14	05	276-281
		14	06	332-340
		15	05	288-295
		15	06	361
		17	07	391-395
		18	03	136-141
		19	03	100-106
		19	04	170-173
		22	02	68-73
		23	04	199-204
		26	01	36-47
		27	02	78-90
	parish system	21	01	4-10
	parliamentary records	04	08	307-314
	plate and vestments	07	07	219-222
	political affiliations	23	02	103-110
	politics and religion 1918-45	28	03	159-175
	proofs of age	05	07	224-230
	protestation returns	02	08	251

INDEX OF SUBJECTS

subject	sub-heading	vol	no	pages
religious history *(cont.)*	protestation returns *(cont.)*	04	05	182-184
		14	03	134-141
	Quakers	03	02	55-61
		08	07	258-262
		21	02	70-75
	rates for repewing	22	04	203-207
	recent work (1969)	08	07	237-242
	recusancy	06	08	266-269
		15	05	288-295
	Reformation in Bristol	28	01	3-15
	Reformation, consequences	07	08	253-257
	regional differences 1851	27	04	194-217
	registration of oaths	02	11	337-339
	religious returns 1829	17	08	483-489
		18	04	162-167
	research topics	08	07	237-242
	round church towers	08	08	282-287
	saints' days and festivals	01	06	182-185
	secularism and atheism	08	06	221-227
	social activities	25	02	95-108
	social role of chapel	10	05	253-258
	sources	08	04	131-134
		09	03	115-120
	sports teams	25	02	95-108
	St Helena	28	02	108-122
	teacher training	12	03-04	161-166
	temperance movement	08	04	135-138
		08	05	180-186
	terminology	02	01	15-18
	theological conflict	21	03	120-125
	tithes	01	12	361-364
		14	01	24-27
	Victorian churches	21	03	120-125
		27	02	91-105
	Victorian Whitby	28	03	78-93
	visitation records	02	01	19-22
		07	01	17-27
	wafer ovens	07	05	161-16
	wartime pacifism	29	02	76-90
	Welsh in Yorkshire	26	04	223-236
removal orders		05	04	111-114
		12	03-04	136-139
republicanism		27	03	163-182
research techniques	see also *census data; census returns; computing; databases; local history; oral history*			
	analysing literacy	21	01	16-19
	assessment of evidence	18	01	5-12
	biographical material	06	05	163-165
	business histories	06	04	128-133
	calendaring and transcribing	25	01	7-16
	cartographical methods	17	03	135-140
	census analysis	16	05	266-277

INDEX OF SUBJECTS

subject	sub-heading	vol	no	pages
research techniques *(cont.)*	census analysis *(cont.)*	16	06	335-342
		16	08	451-456
		18	02	69-75
	churchyard surveys	13	03	149-159
	community writing	13	05	276-280
	compiling pedigrees	02	12	372-373
	computer simulation	19	02	63-70
	computing	20	03	126-127
		23	01	20-30
		25	04	209-222
		26	02	89-101
	copying documents	02	10	311-312
		05	03	77-79
	data analysis	23	01	20-30
		25	04	209-222
	data handling	16	06	335-342
		25	04	209-222
	data variability	18	03	136-141
	databases	16	05	266-277
		16	08	451-456
		24	02	102-11
		25	02	77-87
		25	04	194-208
		25	04	209-222
		26	02	89-101
		26	04	209-222
		29	01	43-51
	directories, use of	18	04	187-189
	document analysis	13	06	346-348
	document copyright	08	03	106-108
	family reconstitution	06	05	146-150
		06	06	198-203
		09	01	9-15
		25	04	209-222
		27	02	78-90
	field investigations	09	04	183-189
	fieldwork	03	01	1-8
	filing and storing information	02	12	368-372
	general discussion	12	02	67-73
		29	04	256-262
	hedgerow dating	17	06	327-342
	historical databases	20	02	88-89
	house histories	07	06	182-189
	house recording	15	01	6-20
	house repopulation	13	02	86-97
	in US schools	15	04	203-211
	linguistic analysis	28	04	217-224
	newspaper indexing	05	07	212-217
		14	03	143-148
	note-taking	03	06	264-266
	obtaining illustrations	07	02	59-62
	oral history	13	07	408-416

subject	sub-heading	vol	no	pages
research techniques *(cont.)*	oral history *(cont.)*	14	05	284-288
	organising notes	05	01	17-22
	palaeography	01	05	146-154
		03	02	81-94
		07	03	88-91
		16	06	327-334
		26	02	89-101
	photographs, uses of	13	01	23-36
	photography	02	02	41-43
	property research	13	01	11-14
	railway history, writing	08	01	10-15
	record linkages	27	02	78-90
		27	02	130-143
	rural settlement analysis	18	02	69-75
	statistical analyses	22	03	147-150
	transcribing, rules of	07	05	138-145
	VCH methods	22	03	114-127
reservoir construction	Lake District	26	03	155-167
retail price indexes		02	08	235-244
retailing	see also *accounts; business history; commerce and trade; finance and accounting*			
	book trade	26	04	237-245
	cinema proprietors	20	03	118-122
	early modern towns	08	04	118-125
	grocery shop	09	03	126-129
	inventory evidence	04	06	227-231
	licensed trade	17	08	457-464
		25	01	31-42
	pawnbroking	20	01	24-30
	Pitt's shop tax	14	06	348-351
	probate valuations	16	08	467-477
	shop tax	14	06	348-351
	stationers	26	04	237-245
	trade tokens	06	01	2-8
		06	02	55-62
	urban 1800-1950	29	03	167-182
	Wolverhampton 1800-1950	29	03	167-182
Richmond Philanthropic Society		27	03	144-162
ridge and furrow		05	01	23-28
		07	03	95-98
rivers	nomenclature	12	06	273-277
roads and highways	ancient	12	05	212-220
	boundary markers	18	02	58-64
	bridges and fords	07	08	250-252
	Bristol bridges	25	02	66-76
	bus services	13	05	280-289
		15	04	221-225
	cartographic evidence	12	05	212-220
	charabanc traffic	24	04	217-224
	coaching services	14	06	341-346
		15	06	338-344
	conditions of	01	04	102-106

INDEX OF SUBJECTS

subject	sub-heading	vol	no	pages
roads and highways (cont.)	county councils	23	01	31-39
	documentary evidence	12	05	212-220
	enclosure roads	25	02	77-87
	footpaths	01	03	73-77
	highway surveyors	01	10	301-304
		06	04	110-114
	in 18th c	15	06	338-344
	maps and plans	08	02	61-71
	motor vehicles	17	06	351-357
	parochial administration	27	01	3-17
	place-names	07	08	250-252
	Roman	04	07	282-290
		12	05	212-220
	route villages	19	04	162-166
	surveyors' accounts	01	10	301-304
	tolls	01	04	102-106
	turnpikes	02	01	4-7
		05	02	39-43
		07	03	84-87
		15	06	338-344
Rockingham potteries		24	01	37-43
Roman period	bibliographies	01	07	209-212
	centuriation	03	01	9-12
	inscriptions	02	10	289-292
	roads	04	07	282-290
		12	05	212-220
rope-making	Isle of Man	10	07	332-333
Royal Commission on Historical Monuments		07	03	92-4
		10	07	344-350
royalty	descent of Crown	02	02	49
	hospital patrons	24	01	15-26
	hunting reserves	03	07	305-307
	letters patent	01	02	47-51
	pubs named after	12	01	31-35
rural settlement	see also *agricultural history; agriculture; architecture; buildings; estate management; landscape history; manorial history; occupations and employment; population and demography; villages*			
	administration	27	01	3-17
	agricultural communities	09	04	178-183
	agricultural unions	13	05	259-262
	agriculture	04	08	338-345
	Angus (Scotland)	15	08	456-463
	apprenticeships	08	07	232-236
		14	07	400-406
	bibliographies	07	01	7-13
		16	05	260-265
	bus services	13	05	280-289
	census analysis	15	01	25-32
		18	02	69-75
	change in 19th c	17	04	199-204
	class structure	06	08	271-278
	closed villages	15	01	25-33

subject	sub-heading	vol	no	pages
rural settlement *(cont.)*	community, idea of	26	01	36-47
	cottages	10	07	327-332
	depopulation	03	05	185-189
	deserted villages	02	07	193-196
		13	08	471-474
	Domesday evidence	01	09	261-264
		01	10	297-300
		01	11	344-347
	education	15	08	474-477
	electoral registers	11	01	30-34
	employment structure 19th c	27	03	130-143
	enclosure land sales	12	07	337-341
	encroachments on waste	11	03	141-147
	estate maps and plans	07	07	223-231
	estate villages	14	01	35-43
		16	01	4-14
	farming, 19th c	03	07	292-298
	field books	15	02	67-69
	field-names	13	07	388-396
	hearth tax	11	07	385-389
	housing styles	16	06	323-326
	hundred rolls	05	01	9-16
	idea of 'country'	26	01	36-47
		27	04	i-xx
	industrial colonies	23	03	146-154
	land tax evidence	07	01	7-13
	lead-mining	18	03	112-118
	linguistics and social structure	28	04	217-224
	manorial system	01	03	82-85
	migration	04	01	9-11
	moated sites	05	02	34-38
	model communities	16	01	4-14
	open field systems	04	02	73-77
		05	01	23-28
	open villages	26	01	16-35
	parish libraries	15	07	406-413
	parish records	06	04	110-114
	paupers	16	01	15-20
	peasants	11	04	200-206
	place-name evidence	22	03	114-127
	plague in	14	06	332-340
	planned villages	09	05	233-241
	population mobility	27	04	i-xx
	reading rooms	20	04	155-157
	recent research (1982)	15	03	157-160
	route villages	19	04	162-6
	sanitary provision	21	04	156-161
	Scotland 17th c	15	08	456-463
	social classes (medieval)	05	01	9-16
	social mobility	15	08	456-463
	social structure 17th 18th c	28	04	194-207
	sources (general)	07	01	7-13

INDEX OF SUBJECTS

subject	sub-heading	vol	no	pages
rural settlement *(cont.)*	tithe accounts	14	01	24-27
	total history	10	08	398-401
	trades and crafts	08	07	232-236
		28	03	145-158
	travellers' descriptions	10	01	27-32
	village communities	06	08	271-278
	village destruction	28	04	208-216
	village morphology	09	05	233-241
	village origins	06	05	166-168
	village shops	09	03	126-129
	water supplies	26	03	155-167
	yeoman farmers	26	01	16-35
saints' days	calendar of	01	06	182-185
sale catalogues	local history value	13	03	131-139
salt industry	place-name evidence	07	05	146-149
sanitation	rural communities	21	04	156-161
school managers		10	06	277-281
school boards		09	03	130-134
schools	see also *education (current); education history*			
	absenteeism	15	08	474-477
	agricultural depression	15	08	474-477
	archives	01	08	230-233
		12	03-04	161-166
		17	08	490-493
		18	01	21-22
		29	02	102-113
	archives, use in	07	02	47-52
		19	01	16-17
	charity	24	03	145-152
	church records	05	02	44-50
	citations	15	06	355-357
	grammar	15	03	137-143
	histories	01	08	230-233
	history exhibition	02	05	149-150
	in 19th c	15	03	137-143
	industrial schools	13	02	74-78
	informal education	11	08	473-476
	inventory evidence	04	08	320-324
	local history in	07	02	47-52
		12	05	223-228
		12	08	403-407
		13	03	140-145
		13	05	290-296
		18	04	174-182
		21	03	126-30
	local history in (US)	15	04	204-211
	logbooks	14	08	471-476
	management and finance	15	03	137-143
	managers' records	10	06	277-281
	open air	29	02	102-113
	parliamentary records	04	08	307-314
	reformatories	13	02	74-78

INDEX OF SUBJECTS

subject	sub-heading	vol	no	pages
schools *(cont.)*	registers	04	01	29-33
	rural communities	15	08	474-477
	sources for	29	02	102-113
	straw-plaiting	19	03	107-113
	teaching packs for	13	07	425-430
	Scotland	17	01	11-18
schoolteachers	bishops' licences	05	01	2-6
	inventories	04	08	320-324
	social origins	12	03-04	161-166
	training	12	03-04	161-166
		16	04	204-206
		21	04	162-167
	Victorian	15	03	137-143
science and technology	agricultural research	23	02	85-91
	bibliography	04	06	245-250
	mining in 19th c	23	04	188-198
	surveying	23	04	218-227
Scotland	National Library	11	08	445-448
Scottish National Portrait Gallery		11	07	382-384
Scottish Protestant League		27	02	106-117
Scottish Record Office		09	07	353-356
	estate records	14	01	35-43
	general description	11	03	123-129
sculpture and carving	architectural	10	06	301-302
	churchyard monuments	16	07	412-417
	early Christian	04	04	140-142
	Early English	04	05	198-201
	fonts	23	03	130-145
	gravestones	06	07	229-233
	Lincoln Cathedral	24	02	83-90
	monuments	02	10	297-303
	Scottish graveyards	23	02	66-84
	slate headstones	08	06	213-217
	sundials and scratchdials	17	08	465-474
	war memorials	20	03	123-125
		26	04	209-222
seaside resorts	see also *leisure and entertainment; tourism; urban history*			
	archive sources	13	06	323-331
	Blackpool	24	04	194-205
	Bournemouth	10	03	126-134
	conference	14	05	270-275
	early guidebooks	05	06	183-188
	newspaper evidence	13	06	323-331
	parks and gardens	20	04	158-165
	photograph	17	02	113
	pleasure gardens	03	08	319-324
	Scottish	24	04	206-216
		29	04	240-255
	Spanish	24	02	91-101
	visitor numbers	23	04	205-216
		29	04	240-255
	visitors to	13	06	323-331

subject	sub-heading	vol	no	pages
seaside resorts *(cont.)*	wartime experiences	29	04	240-255
	Weston-super-Mare	20	04	158-165
	Whitby	28	02	78-93
sectarianism		15	07	388-401
secularism		08	06	221-2227
Selden Society		01	07	220-224
self-help	building societies	10	02	65-69
	friendly societies	16	03	161-167
	poverty in Bristol 1816	25	01	17-30
sequestration records		24	01	4-14
servants		02	11	334-336
		29	02	66-75
settlement	laws of	02	09	268-270
	certificates	12	03-04	136-139
	removal orders	05	04	111-114
settlement patterns	central place theory	21	03	99-108
sewerage and drainage		14	04	202-210
sheriffs	Scotland	03	08	329-331
ships and shipping		05	06	177-182
	Aquitainia at Liverpool	16	04	234
	Clyde ferries	24	04	206-216
	Forth ferries	24	04	206-216
	medieval wool trade	22	01	18-40
	Muslim merchant seamen	27	04	225-244
	Rain's Sunderland plan	17	07	417-422
	St Helena	28	02	108-122
	taxation records 18th c	28	02	66-77
shop tax		14	06	348-351
shops and shopping	see *business history; commerce and trade; retailing*			
Shropshire Records & Research Centre		26	03	168-174
silk industry		12	03-04	152-156
slavery		19	01	8-15
smallholders		11	04	200-206
smallholdings		17	01	31-38
social history	see also *agricultural history; archive sources; commerce and trade; crime and punishment; education history; family and kinship; law and order; leisure and entertainment; sport and recreation; urban history*			
	bibliography	11	08	449-451
	car ownership	17	06	351-357
	church courts	04	01	12-22
	cinemas	20	03	118-122
	Civil War	01	01	13-17
	clothing	29	01	3-13
	community leisure	16	05	supp
	crime and deprivation	15	02	74-79
	definition of community	26	01	36-47
	demography	14	05	276-281
	deposition evidence	17	05	269-276
	drinking and pubs	25	01	31-42
	early motoring	17	06	351-357
	folk music	12	01	13-17
	friendly societies	03	03	95-101

subject	sub-heading	vol	no	pages
social history *(cont.)*	geographical segregation	21	04	168-176
	guidebooks	05	06	183-188
	hundred rolls	05	01	9-16
	influential personalities	15	07	388-401
	inns and public houses	02	05	134-137
		06	01	18-21
	local history and	10	08	390-394
	London Gazette as source	15	04	212-217
	medical care	20	04	173-86
	moated sites	05	02	34-38
	music hall	09	08	379-386
	newspapers	11	06	321-326
	parish magazines	16	08	457-466
	photographs	15	08	468-473
	photographs as source	13	01	22-36
	popular movements 18th c	04	06	235-241
	proofs of age	05	07	224-230
	pub names	12	01	31-35
	public baths	25	03	142-152
	recent developments (1976)	12	03-04	131-135
	religious conflict	21	03	120-125
	social surveys	20	02	109-117
	valentine cards	09	03	134-141
	Wales	11	08	449-451
social structure	Battersea politics	27	03	163-182
	garden villages	27	01	30-47
	immigrant communities	28	04	225-241
	oral evidence 1945-1970	28	04	i-xvi
	philanthropy and	25	01	17-30
	population mobility	27	04	i-xx
	rural communities 17th c	28	04	194-207
	peasants and smallholders	11	04	200-206
societies and organisations	Agricultural History, Institute of	19	01	18-20
	archive collecting by	21	01	11-15
	British & Foreign Schools Society	16	04	204-206
	British Assoc. for Local History	22	02	74-83
		22	02	89-96
	British Optical Association	02	11	330-333
	British Records Association	03	07	283-285
	British Union of Fascists	27	02	106-117
	Business Archives Council	06	04	128-133
	Cambridge Group Hist Population	06	06	198-203
		07	06	178-181
		20	02	88-89
	Chambers of Commerce	16	01	36-48
	Charity Organisation Society	21	03	109-119
		21	04	147-154
		23	01	45
	Conf Regional and Local Historians	28	03	176-179
	Deserted Medieval Village Res Group	02	07	193-196
	Electrical Association for Women	28	02	94-107
	English Place Name Society	02	02	44-47

subject	sub-heading	vol	no	pages
societies and organisations *(cont.)*	English Place Name Society *(cont.)*	07	05	146-149
		22	03	114-127
	Genealogists, Society of	01	03	70-73
		22	02	68-73
	Guernsey	21	01	20-25
	Heralds, College of	02	12	362-365
	History & Computing, Ass for	20	02	88-89
	Incorporated Church Building Soc	27	02	91-105
	Institute of Historical Research	22	03	128-137
	Lincoln Record Society	06	05	157-162
	local history	01	01	30-33
		01	07	202-205
		01	10	305-308
		02	07	212-214
		02	09	274-275
		03	03	126-129
		14	03	131-133
		15	08	491-492
		22	02	58-67
		26	01	3-14
	local history (Sussex)	12	06	267-273
	local political 1918-45	28	03	159-175
	Loughton Mutual Labor-Aid Soc	24	04	229-242
	membership (historical)	26	01	3-14
	Monumental Brass Society	01	05	159-162
	National Register of Archives	01	04	127-129
	National Reg of Archives Scotland	01	12	374-377
		17	01	11-18
	National Secular Society	08	06	221-227
	National Trust	26	02	80-88
	National Trust Scotland	25	04	223-230
	Northumberland Ass Loc Hist Socs	26	04	209-222
	Prudent Man's Friendly Society	25	01	17-30
	publications by	12	06	277-83
		12	07	343-348
	Railway & Canal Historical Soc	02	09	257-260
	regional family history	13	02	100-102
	Richmond Philanthropic Society	27	03	144-162
	Royal Comm Historical Monuments	07	03	92-4
	Selden Society	01	07	220-224
	self-help	24	04	229-242
	South Derbyshire Research Group	26	02	89-101
	Standing Conf for Local History	01	12	371-373
		22	02	89-96
	transactions series	09	01	16-22
	transport history	02	09	257-260
	Womens Institute	28	03	159-175
	Workers Education Association	02	01	8-11
		05	03	81-84
		22	02	58-67
	Yorkshire Archaeological Society	19	04	170-173
Society of Friends		21	02	70-75

subject	sub-heading	vol	no	pages
Society of Friends *(cont.)*	archives	03	02	55-61
		08	07	258-262
sociology	influence in local history	26	01	36-47
	village communities	06	08	271-278
South Derbyshire Research Group		26	02	89-101
Southampton Institute of Education		06	07	218-222
spas	Leamington	10	04	186-195
spectacles		02	11	330-333
sport and recreation	see also *customs and traditions; leisure and entertainment*			
	animal cruelty and	10	03	116-124
	cricket	25	02	95-108
	football (interwar)	25	01	31-42
	game shooting	26	03	142-154
	golf	24	04	206-16
	hunting	10	03	116-124
	pleasure gardens	03	08	319-324
	recreation rooms	16	05	supp
	resort development	24	04	206-216
	Shrovetide football	14	05	292
	street-names	16	04	195-203
	tourism and	29	04	240-255
	water sports (Windermere)	24	04	217-224
squatting		03	07	305-307
	encroachments on waste	11	03	141-147
stagecoaches		14	06	341-346
stamp duty	probate inventories	16	08	467-477
Standing Conference for Local History		01	12	371-373
		22	02	89-96
	Blake Report	13	08	451-456
Star Chamber		04	03	89-94
		17	07	408-416
statistics	computer analysis	19	02	63-70
	demographic analyses	09	01	27-35
	methodology debated	22	03	147-150
	reliability of	09	01	9-15
		14	05	276-281
		16	03	156-160
steel-making		13	06	349-352
		29	04	223-230
Stirling Journal	indexing project	14	03	143-148
stocking frame-knitting		28	01	24-35
stocks and pillories		03	06	231-236
stonemasons		02	08	232-234
		21	02	60-65
	monuments	02	10	297-303
	slate headstones	08	06	213-217
	styles	16	07	412-417
street-names		01	09	278-282
	Ethiopian influence	14	08	468-469
	gate	08	08	288-291
	general	16	04	195-203
	imperial themes	22	02	84-88

subject	sub-heading	vol	no	pages
street-names *(cont.)*	medieval	16	04	195-203
strikes	agricultural workers	11	03	134-141
	colliery photograph	16	05	298
	Durham coalfield	16	07	418-424
	General Strike	16	01	36-48
		16	02	83-89
	lead-mining	17	02	101-106
subterranean passages		02	02	33-36
suburban development	auction catalogues	13	03	131-139
	elite Victorian	15	05	259-271
	garden villages	27	01	30-47
	general	04	07	275-281
	inter-war	11	01	24-29
	local politics	11	05	285-289
	maps and plans	07	06	196-208
	public transport	13	05	280-289
	relict hedgerows	18	02	65-68
	street-names	16	04	195-203
	Victorian	10	04	186-195
suffrage movement		11	02	77-79
Sun Fire Office		09	01	3-8
		17	03	141-9
sundials		17	08	465-474
surgeons	bishops' licences	05	01	2-6
surnames	census evidence	12	02	93-101
	civil registration	27	04	i-xx
	computing	27	04	i-xx
	diffusion	17	07	391-395
		19	02	63-70
		20	02	65-72
	distribution	16	07	392-404
		20	01	3-8
	family history	02	04	114-116
	family stability	26	01	36-47
	feet of fines	24	02	66-82
	genealogy	04	02	56-61
		07	06	178-181
	geographical origins	17	07	391-395
	habitual territories	26	01	36-47
	hearth tax evidence	27	04	i-xx
	heredity of	10	04	171-177
	Latin forms	01	12	368-371
	local history	27	04	i-xx
	locative	10	01	3-7
		10	04	171-177
		10	05	227-233
		13	02	80-86
		27	04	i-xx
	medieval	13	02	80-86
	migration	14	01	35-43
	minor place-names	10	01	3-7
	nicknames	27	04	i-xx

subject	sub-heading	vol	no	pages
surnames *(cont.)*	occupational	10	04	171-177
		27	04	i-xx
	origin	27	04	i-xx
	patronymic	17	07	405-407
	personal names	27	04	i-xx
	place-loyalty	16	06	343-345
	population mobility	13	02	80-86
		08	08	299-302
	publications	09	07	357-361
	stability	12	01	3-6
		16	06	343-345
	survey project	08	08	299-302
	telephone directories	16	07	392-404
		27	04	i-xx
	topographical	27	04	i-xx
	Welsh	07	06	189-191
		17	07	405-407
		25	03	178-183
	Yorkshire	10	04	171-177
survey techniques	housing	15	01	6-20
surveying	boundaries	18	02	58-64
	enclosure maps	07	08	265-274
	estate maps	07	07	223-231
	in 18th c	23	04	218-227
	photographic	20	04	166-172
	tithe maps	07	08	265-274
surveyors	enclosure	29	01	25-42
surveys	architectural	15	01	6-20
tables	Victorian leg-coverings	18	04	162-167
taxation and rates	see also *accounts; business history; commerce and trade; finance and accounting; tithes*			
	bibliography (tithes)	07	08	265-274
	church courts	04	01	12-22
	Civil War	20	03	128-136
		22	03	138-143
		22	04	191-202
	coal-mining evidence	18	01	5-12
	commerce and trade	28	02	66-77
	Domesday Survey	01	09	261-264
	Hearth Tax	04	05	182-184
		27	04	i-xx
		28	04	194-207
	highway rates	01	10	301-304
	highway tolls	01	04	102-106
		02	01	4-7
		05	02	39-43
		07	03	84-87
	income tax 1803	13	06	332-338
	land tax	06	05	152-156
		07	01	7-13
		07	06	182-189
		28	02	66-77

subject	sub-heading	vol	no	pages
taxation and rates *(cont.)*	lay subsidies	03	07	271-278
		03	08	325-328
		04	03	101-109
		04	04	129-133
	manorial dues	29	03	130-151
	maritime history	28	02	66-77
	militia rates	26	03	130-141
	poll tax	03	07	271-278
		17	05	277-280
	poor rates	01	09	269-272
	rate books	17	05	277-280
		18	03	136-141
	ratepayer parsimony	26	03	155-167
	record linkages	27	02	78-90
	regional income levels	13	06	332-338
	stamp duty	16	08	467-477
	surname studies	27	04	i-xx
	taxation 18th c	28	02	66-77
	tithes	01	12	361-364
		02	12	353-356
		03	07	292-298
		04	01	12-22
		17	04	205-211
		18	03	136-141
		25	01	7-16
		26	01	16-35
	urban data 18th c	28	02	66-77
	vehicle licensing	17	06	351-357
telegraph service		24	03	153-163
telephone directories	surname evidence	16	07	392-404
		20	01	3-8
		27	04	i-xx
temperance movement	research issues	08	05	180-186
	sources for	08	04	135-138
tenancy	agreements	01	01	5-8
	auction catalogues	13	03	131-139
	farm sale evidence	28	01	36-49
	game laws	26	03	142-154
	garden villages	27	01	30-47
	inquisitions post mortem	01	03	77-81
	leasehold procedures	16	03	156-160
	manorial	18	01	16-18
	plea rolls	01	05	155-158
	probate evidence	16	04	217-227
	social structure and	28	04	194-207
terriers		01	12	361-364
textile industry	building plans	19	01	3-7
	inventory evidence	04	06	227-231
	medieval cloth trade	22	01	18-40
	workers' housing	23	03	146-154
textiles	clothing 18th c	29	01	3-13
	prices and valuations	16	08	467-477

subject	sub-heading	vol	no	pages
theatre	pleasure gardens	03	08	319-324
	sources	06	01	22-24
	Shakespeare, William	07	02	42-46
Thomason Tracts		05	05	141-144
timber	hundred rolls	20	02	73-79
	parkland	03	08	332-349
	wood products	20	02	73-79
	woodland management	27	02	66-77
timber trade	Yorkshire	16	02	73-82
tithes		01	12	361-364
	bibliography	07	08	265-274
	church courts	04	01	12-22
		25	01	7-16
	field-names	02	12	353-356
	field patterns	03	07	292-298
	files	17	04	205-211
	land use evidence	26	01	16-35
	parson's accounts	13	07	397-405
	sources, variability	18	03	136-141
tithings		27	01	3-17
title deeds		06	03	86-90
		07	06	182-189
	feet of fines	01	01	5-8
		24	02	66-82
	plea rolls	01	05	155-158
toll houses		01	04	102-106
		02	01	4-7
		05	02	39-43
tourism	see also *leisure and entertainment; seaside resorts; urban history*			
	American visitors	29	04	240-255
	Blackpool	24	04	194-205
	census: visitor numbers	23	04	205-216
	conference report	26	03	175-177
	early guidebooks	05	06	183-188
	early travellers	03	01	20-31
	excursions 19th c	26	02	66-79
	heritage issues	25	04	223-230
	inland resorts	13	06	323-331
		24	04	217-224
	middle-class	24	04	217-224
	Scotland	29	04	240-255
	seaside resorts	03	08	319-324
		05	06	183-188
		13	06	323-331
		17	02	113
		20	04	158-165
		23	04	205-216
		24	02	91-101
		24	04	194-205
		24	04	206-216
		28	02	78-93
		29	04	240-255

INDEX OF SUBJECTS

subject	sub-heading	vol	no	pages
tourism *(cont.)*	Spanish internal	24	02	91-101
	Victorian Whitby	28	02	78-93
	vulnerability to economic change	29	04	240-255
	wartime problems of tourist trade	29	04	240-255
	Windermere	24	04	217-224
tournaments		04	02	78-80
town planning	see also *estate management; landscape history; urban history*			
	building plans	19	01	3-7
	garden cities	17	01	31-38
	garden villages	27	01	30-47
	immigrant communities and	28	04	225-241
	parks and gardens	20	04	158-165
	Victorian Whitby	28	02	78-93
town plans		07	06	196-208
		07	07	223-231
	Ordnance Survey	05	08	251-259
towns	see also *seaside resorts; urban history*			
	bibliography	16	02	67-72
	book trade	26	04	237-245
	borough administration	02	10	293-296
	borough records	02	09	265-267
	building plans	19	01	3-7
		19	03	120-123
	communities within (19th c)	29	04	223-230
	data sources	18	03	136-141
	development 17th c	20	03	128-136
	development 20th c	20	03	109-117
	early guidebooks	05	06	183-188
	economic activity 17th c	20	03	128-136
	garden cities	27	01	30-47
	growth 1570-1770	08	04	118-125
	histories	01	10	308-311
	industrial	02	05	146-148
	late medieval decline	29	04	194-211
	maps and plans	07	06	196-208
	market trading	20	03	128-136
		29	04	194-211
	medieval boroughs	02	11	321-325
		29	04	194-211
	medieval Bristol	28	01	3-15
	medieval charters	02	11	321-325
	medieval markets	29	04	194-211
	overcrowding	16	03	156-160
	population statistics	20	03	128-136
	ports	05	06	177-182
	poverty in	25	01	17-30
	primary towns	11	05	263-277
	street-names	16	04	195-203
	suburban development	04	07	275-281
	trade and town development	29	04	194-211
	transport themes	07	03	84-87
trade tokens		06	01	2-7

subject	sub-heading	vol	no	pages
trade tokens *(cont.)*		06	02	55-61
trade unions		04	05	177-181
	agricultural	13	05	259-262
		13	06	353-359
	anti-semitism in	27	02	106-117
	Durham miners	16	07	418-424
	frame knitters (1810s)	28	01	24-35
	General Strike	16	01	36-48
		16	02	83-89
	histories of	01	09	273-277
	local political influence 1918-45	28	03	159-175
	local politics and	27	03	163-182
	racial prejudice in	27	04	225-244
	sources	01	09	273-277
		04	05	177-181
		20	03	109-117
	trades councils	03	04	160-165
trades and crafts	see also *agricultural history; business history; industrial history; occupations and employment*			
	apprenticeships	02	12	357-361
		08	07	232-236
	book trade	26	04	237-245
	building trade	22	01	41-42
	cutlers	25	04	194-208
		29	04	223-230
	directory evidence	13	04	205-209
		17	06	343-350
	equipment valuations	16	08	467-477
	graffiti evidence	23	01	4-19
	inventory valuations	16	08	467-477
	midwifery	23	03	163-169
	place-names	08	01	16-21
	stonemasons	16	07	412-417
		21	02	60-65
		23	02	66-84
	straw-plaiting	19	03	107-113
	street-naming	16	04	195-203
	symbols on gravestones	23	02	66-84
	timber industry	20	02	73-79
	urban 17th c	20	03	128-136
	urban growth	08	06	196-204
	Victorian Hertfordshire	28	03	145-158
	women in 18th c	17	03	158-162
trades councils		03	04	160-165
transcribing	rules for	07	05	138-145
transhumance	pre-Conquest evidence	27	01	18-29
transport	see also *canals and navigations; coaching services; railways; roads and highways*			
	access to resorts	24	04	206-216
	archives	04	08	329-334
	bibliographies	04	03	116-119
	bus services	13	05	280-289

subject	sub-heading	vol	no	pages
transport *(cont.)*	coalfield schemes	16	07	418-424
	General Strike	16	02	83-89
	medieval wool trade	04	04	134-139
	place-names	07	08	250-252
	port towns	02	07	207-211
	postal services	29	03	152-166
	railway histories	05	01	17-22
	research topics	07	03	84-87
	settlement and	19	04	162-166
travellers		19	04	162-166
	bibliography	08	06	196-204
	journals	03	01	20-31
	local history and	06	02	38-44
treasure	coin hoards	06	01	2-7
turnips	introduction of	04	01	1-7
turnpike roads		01	04	102-106
		02	01	4-7
		05	02	39-43
		05	02	39-43
		07	03	84-87
unemployment	local politics of	27	03	163-182
	servants	02	11	334-336
universities	Chancery proceedings	06	08	254-259
	college accounts	28	01	16-23
	local history in	13	02	67-80
		13	08	451-456
urban history	see also *architecture; buildings; town planning; towns*			
	archaeological surveys	08	04	139-145
	auction catalogues	13	03	131-139
	bibliography	16	02	67-72
	bibliography (medieval)	16	05	260-265
	book trade	26	04	237-245
	borough accounts	02	10	293-296
	borough creation (medieval)	29	04	194-211
	borough records	02	09	265-267
		29	04	194-211
	building plans	19	01	3-7
		19	03	120-123
	bus services	13	05	280-289
	cemeteries 19th c	28	03	130-144
	census evidence	18	03	119-126
		29	04	223-230
	census reliability	23	04	205-216
	charity and philanthropy	27	03	144-162
	community identification	29	04	223-230
	constituencies 1867	13	07	416-424
	data sources	18	03	136-141
	deposition evidence	17	05	269-276
	development 17th c	20	03	128-136
	directories	13	04	205-209
		17	06	343-350
		18	04	187-189

subject	sub-heading	vol	no	pages
urban history *(cont.)*	early guidebooks	05	06	183-188
	feet of fines	24	02	66-82
	fire insurance records	17	03	141-149
	garden cities	27	01	30-47
	growth 1570-1770	08	04	118-125
	immigrant communities	28	04	225-241
	industrial colonies	23	03	146-154
		29	04	223-230
	industries 20th c	16	03	146-150
	late medieval decline	29	04	194-211
	Local Boards of Health	21	04	168-176
	market halls	08	04	118-125
	market towns	20	03	128-136
		29	04	194-211
	marriage patterns 19th c	29	04	223-230
	mechanics' institutes	07	02	63-65
	medieval boroughs	02	11	321-325
		29	04	194-211
	medieval Bristol	28	01	3-15
	medieval morphology	16	04	195-203
	micro-studies	18	03	119-126
	Middlesex VCH	23	03	155-162
	models	21	03	99-108
	morphology	20	03	128-136
	non-burghal medieval towns	29	04	194-211
	overcrowding studies	16	03	156-160
	parks and gardens	20	04	158-165
	pauper concentrations	16	01	25-31
	politics, popular	27	03	163-182
	poll tax records	03	07	271-278
	poor and poverty	08	03	98-106
		16	01	25-31
		25	01	17-30
	population sizes	23	04	205-216
		29	04	194-211
	ports	02	07	207-211
	poverty studies	25	01	17-30
	primary towns	11	05	263-277
	property research	13	01	11-14
	public baths	25	03	142-152
	public health reform	21	04	168-176
	Rain's Sunderland plan	17	07	417-422
	residential persistence	29	04	223-230
	resort development	24	04	194-205
		28	02	78-93
		29	04	240-255
	small ports	05	06	177-182
	sources 20th c	20	03	109-117
	Spanish archives	24	02	91-101
	stonemasons	21	02	60-65
	street-names	16	04	195-203
		22	02	84-88

INDEX OF SUBJECTS

subject	sub-heading	vol	no	pages
urban history *(cont.)*	suburban development	04	07	275-281
		18	02	65-68
	suburban maps	07	06	196-208
	taxation 18th c	28	02	66-77
	tourism, dependency on	29	04	240-255
	town plans	05	08	251-259
		07	06	196-208
	trade (medieval)	29	04	194-211
	transport themes	07	03	84-87
	wartime tourism	29	04	240-255
	water supplies	26	03	155-167
vagrancy		02	10	309-310
		21	02	66-69
vestries		06	04	110-114
	administration of poor law	25	03	164-177
	linguistic analysis of records	28	04	217-224
	minutes	01	08	234-237
Victoria County Histories		01	01	2-4
		21	04	146
	current (1992) state	22	03	128-137
	general review	13	01	15-22
	Middlesex	23	03	155-162
villages	see also *rural settlement*			
	change in 19th c	17	04	199-204
	deserted medieval	03	01	1-8
		13	08	471-474
	estate villages	14	01	35-43
		16	01	4-14
	open	26	01	16-35
	open and closed	06	08	271-278
	origins of	06	05	166-168
	route	19	04	162-166
	social structure	06	08	271-278
	sources	07	01	7-13
visitation records		02	01	19-22
		02	03	82-86
		07	01	17-27
wafer ovens		07	05	161-165
wages and salaries	justices' assessments	08	08	293-299
	lead-mining	18	03	112-118
	pottery industry	08	03	78-85
	wage regulation	08	08	293-299
Wales, Great Sessions of		07	06	189-191
war	see also *military history; militia*			
		01	12	371-373
	agriculture during Civil War	29	02	76-90
		01	01	13-17
		02	09	261-264
		21	02	51-59
		22	03	138-143
		22	04	191-202
		26	04	194-208

subject	sub-heading	vol	no	pages
war *(cont.)*	education during	21	04	162-165
	Elizabethan mobilisation	26	03	130-141
	First World War	29	04	240-255
	Guernsey	21	01	20-25
	memorials	20	03	123-125
		26	04	209-222
	military bibliography	16	07	406-411
	military encampments 18th c	29	04	212-222
	popular attitudes to	27	03	163-182
	Second World War	29	02	76-90
	street-names and	22	02	84-88
	tourist trades during	29	04	240-255
war memorials	national survey	20	03	123-125
	recording project	26	04	209-222
waste	common land	07	07	232-240
	Domesday evidence	01	11	344-347
	enclosure from (17th c)	28	04	194-207
	maps of	07	08	265-274
water supplies		26	03	155-167
watermills		02	06	172-175
		02	11	326-329
		07	06	192-195
	locating lost	02	11	326-329
	stream diversions	18	02	58-64
wattle and daub		01	12	365-367
wealth	inventories	28	04	194-207
	lay subsidies	03	08	325-328
		04	03	101-9
weights and measures		02	07	207-211
	land measurement	07	03	95-98
	lead industry	18	03	112-118
	medieval	06	04	115-117
	surveying in 18th c	23	04	218-227
	Tudor construction trade	22	01	41-42
	Welsh	07	05	154-160
Welsh Folk Museum		03	05	197-204
Welsh language	agricultural records	07	05	154-160
	census 1891	22	04	184-190
	genealogical records	07	06	189-191
	place names	25	03	178-185
	probate records	25	03	178-183
	survival among emigrants	26	04	223-236
Whigs		02	03	65-68
William Salt Library (Stafford)		19	03	114-116
wills and inventories	see *probate records*			
windmills		01	02	43-47
		07	06	192-195
wives, sale of		06	06	188-191
women	agricultural workers	27	03	130-143
	bigamy and	24	03	139-144
	building workers	20	02	84-87
	census terminology	13	08	481-487

subject	sub-heading	vol	no	pages
women (cont.)	childbirth	20	01	9-19
	councillors	19	04	159-161
	criminals 19th c	16	05	289-297
	Electrical Association for	28	02	94-107
	family life 1945-1970	28	04	i-xvi
	female pauper apprentices	19	02	51-55
	landladies in resorts	13	06	323-331
	making wills	25	03	178-183
	philanthropic societies	27	03	144-162
	political allegiances	28	03	159-175
	poor relief	25	03	164-177
	radical politics	27	03	163-182
	seating in church	22	04	203-207
	straw-plaiting	19	03	107-113
	traders 18th c	17	03	158-162
	trading activities	24	01	4-14
	wartime tourists	29	04	240-255
	yeoman families	26	01	16-35
women's history	bibliography	17	03	150-157
	co-operative movement	20	03	109-117
	Fawcett Library	23	02	92-97
	feminist sources	23	02	92-97
Women's Institute		28	03	159-175
woodland	botanical evidence	16	02	73-82
	clearance	26	02	66-79
	hedgerow dating	17	06	327-342
	hedgerows	13	04	195-204
	management	27	02	66-77
	management	26	02	66-79
	place-name evidence	16	02	73-82
	South Yorkshire	16	02	73-82
	timber products	20	02	73-79
wool	trade (medieval)	04	04	134-139
		22	01	18-40
	medieval measures	06	04	115-7
Workers Education Association		02	01	8-11
	group projects	22	02	58-67
	publishing	05	03	81-84
workhouses		01	09	269-272
		02	01	11-15
	masters	16	02	93-100
	Royal Hospital, Putney	24	01	15-26
	vagrants	21	02	66-69
working men's clubs		20	04	155-157
Yorkshire Archaeological Society		19	04	170-173

INDEX OF PLACES

This section of the index lists ONLY those places which have been the subject either of a case-study article, or of a shorter but substantive section within a thematic article. It is not intended to be an exhaustive place-name index to the journal. Places in England and Wales are indexed under the appropriate county headings, using pre-1974 county boundaries (including separate entries for London - the pre-1965 LCC area - and Middlesex). Certain larger cities, such as Liverpool and Birmingham, are in addition indexed separately under their own name, as are some regional and district names (e.g. Fylde, Hallamshire) which are similarly included both separately and under the relevant county. There are also separate headings for Wales, Scotland and Ireland, each with subdivisions. After the list for the British Isles a second list covers all other countries and continents.

county/region/city	*town/parish*		*vol*	*no*	*pages*
1.	**British Isles**				
Arden, Forest of		fishponds	07	04	119-126
Bedfordshire	Aspley Guise	poor law in	20	01	9-19
	Harlington	archives	21	01	11-15
	Luton	photographers	19	01	27-29
	Marston Morteyne	poor law in	20	01	9-19
	Northill	poor law in	20	01	9-19
Berkshire		agricultural unions	13	06	353-359
		deposition books	17	05	269-276
		postal services 18th c	29	03	152-166
		topographical place names	12	06	273-277
	Blewbury	village school	06	07	160-166
	Bucklebury	surveying in 18th c	23	04	218-227
	Purley on Thames	boundaries	25	02	88-94
	Reading	cholera	21	04	168-176
Birmingham		business communities	11	08	457-464
		demography 19th c	09	01	27-35
		local history in	02	09	274-275
		modern industries	16	03	146-150
		poor relief	16	01	25-31
		schools	29	02	102-113
		suburban development	15	05	259-271
Black Country		settlement history	18	03	119-126
Blackpool		development late 19th c	24	04	194-205
		Tower	24	04	194-205
		visitor numbers 1921	23	04	205-216
		visitors to	13	06	323-331

INDEX OF PLACES

county/region/city	town/parish		vol	no	pages
Bristol		all-electric house	28	02	94-107
		building industry 19th c	20	02	84-87
		computer databases	29	01	43-51
		diocese of	28	01	3-15
		Electrical Ass for Women	28	02	94-107
		late medieval town	28	01	3-15
		medieval trade	22	01	18-40
		poor relief 1816-1817	25	01	17-30
		riot 1793	25	02	66-76
		training college	12	03-04	161-166
Buckinghamshire		hedgerows	17	06	327-342
		rural settlement	18	02	69-75
	Chesham	church seating	22	04	203-207
	Princes Risborough	enclosure	29	01	25-42
	Swanbourne	agricultural strike	11	03	134-141
	Wolverton	growth of	09	04	190-195
		railway works	17	03	169
Caernarvonshire		Record Office	08	01	22-27
Calder valley		local history publishing	22	02	58-67
Cambridgeshire		Elizabethan militia	26	03	130-141
	Cambridge	trade tokens	06	02	55-61
	Foxton	*The Common Stream*	12	08	391-394
	Melbourn	house repopulation	13	02	86-97
	Sawston	agricultural glossary	04	07	291-295
Cardiganshire [Ceredigion]		agriculture 19th c	09	04	178-183
Cheshire		agriculture 19th c	13	05	270-276
		antiquarians 19th c	26	01	3-14
		book trade pre-1850	26	04	237-245
		labourers' wages	08	08	293-299
	Barnton		06	05	163-165
	Bromborough	census analysis	16	05	266-277
	Chester	booksellers	26	04	237-245
		diocese of	11	01	14-17
	Congleton	industrial structure	12	03-04	152-156
	Macclesfield	book trade	26	04	237-245
		silk industry	12	03-04	152-156
	Stockport	book trade	26	04	237-245
	Wallasey	college of further edn	20	01	20-23
	Wybunbury	estate sizes	11	04	200-206
Chilterns		woodland	20	02	73-79
Cornwall		pre-Conquest charters	27	01	18-29
	Mawgan Porth	archaeological excavation	01	05	134-139
	Polbathic	maps of (critique)	17	03	135-140
		recreation rooms	16	05	supp
Cumberland		parishes and townships	27	01	3-17
	Cleator Moor	industrial housing	23	03	146-154
Cumbria	Lake District	reservoir construction	26	03	155-167
		tourism in 1920s	24	04	217-224
		visitor numbers	23	04	205-216
Denbighshire		game laws 19th c	26	03	142-154
	Abergele	public health	14	04	202-210
Derbyshire		civil unrest, medieval	15	07	388-401

county/region/city	town/parish		vol	no	pages
Derbyshire *(cont.)*		farm sale advertisements	28	01	36-49
		open field systems	04	02	73-77
		religious returns 1829	18	04	162-167
		rural social structures	28	04	194-207
	Ashbourne	Georgian buildings	14	02	68-75
			14	03	149-155
		Shrovetide football	14	05	292
		society in 19th c	15	07	388-401
	Bowden Middlecale	rural social structure	28	04	194-207
	Church Gresley	inventory analysis	26	02	89-101
	Cromford	early industry	09	04	183-189
	Derby	architecture 1699	26	02	102-114
		Georgian houses	14	02	68-75
	Ilkeston	bus services	15	04	221-224
	Peak	royal forest of	28	04	194-207
	Stanton in the Peak	early charter	13	04	209-216
Devonshire		pre-Conquest charters	27	01	18-29
		small ports	05	06	177-182
	Dawlish	local history	11	03	162-166
	Devonport	overcrowding in	16	03	156-160
	Exeter	crime 19th c	16	05	289-297
		underground conduits	02	02	33-36
	Torquay		05	06	177-182
Dorset		farmers' inventories	12	05	228-234
	Blandford Forum	fire of 1734	10	08	385-389
		Bridport	15	06	358-360
	Poole	18th century taxation	28	02	66-77
	Sherborne	castle estate	25	04	231-241
Durham, County		agriculture in 19th c	17	04	205-211
		coalfield	16	07	418-424
		photographs discussed	13	01	22-36
		women's political views	28	03	159-175
	Barnard Castle	social deprivation	15	02	74-79
	Byers Green	village morphology	09	05	233-241
	South Shields	early 20th c migration	27	04	225-244
		photographers	19	04	174-176
	Stockton-on Tees	dispensary	10	05	221-226
	Sunderland	Rain's 1785 plan	17	07	417-422
Edinburgh			24	01	4-14
		archive repositories	09	07	353-356
		Scottish archives	01	12	374-377
Essex		apprenticeships	14	07	400-406
		archives	13	04	217-223
		bigamy among poor	24	03	139-144
		final concords	14	07	411-416
		military encampments	29	04	212-222
		plague	14	06	332-340
		rural unrest in	03	02	49-54
	Colchester	women traders 18th c	17	03	158-162
	Cressing Temple	barns	27	02	66-77
	Earls Colne	church	27	02	91-105
	Great Oakley	plague	14	06	332-340

county/region/city	town/parish		vol	no	pages
Essex (cont.)	Loughton	self-help movement	24	04	229-242
	Saffron Walden	libraries	25	03	153-163
	Upminster	publishing history	04	03	110-115
	Witham	medieval market town	29	04	194-211
Flintshire		game laws 19th c	26	03	142-154
	Mostyn	migration from	26	04	223-236
	St. Deiniol	library	23	01	40-44
Furness		communities and society	26	01	36-47
Fylde		hearth tax and settlement	11	07	385-389
		parishes and townships	27	01	3-17
Glamorganshire		local history organisations	14	02	91-92
	Aberavon	public health	14	04	202-210
	Merthyr Tydfil	public health	14	04	202-210
		traditional housing	18	04	162-167
	St. Fagans	folk museum	03	05	197-207
	Swansea	oral history project	14	05	284-288
Gloucestershire		parish councils	17	04	212-218
		travellers' descriptions	10	01	27-32
	Ashley	manorial customs	15	03	166-173
	Bledington	cottages	10	07	327-332
	Bristol	all-electric house	28	02	94-107
		building industry 19th c	20	02	84-87
		computer databases	29	01	43-51
		diocese of	28	01	3-15
		Electrical Ass for Women	28	02	94-107
		late medieval town	28	01	3-15
		medieval trade	22	01	18-40
		poor relief 1816-1817	25	01	17-30
		riot 1793	25	02	66-76
	Bristol (Fishponds)	training college	12	03-04	161-166
	Cheltenham	manorial customs	15	03	166-173
		topographical poetry	17	03	163-168
		travellers' descriptions	10	01	27-32
	Gloucester	travellers' descriptions	10	01	27-32
	Iron Acton	village library	19	04	147-158
	Painswick	parish councillors	17	04	212-219
	Standish	churchyard	16	07	412-417
	Stonehouse	churchyard	16	07	412-417
	Stroud	boundary markers	18	02	58-64
Guernsey		local history	21	01	20-25
Hallamshire		cutlers' apprentices	25	04	194-208
		population mobility	27	04	i-xx
Hampshire	Bournemouth	development of	10	03	126-134
	Sopley		07	04	112-118
	Southampton	urban growth 1878-1914	12	07	353-359
	Warnford	paper-making	08	02	42-46
	Winchester		04	01	12-22
		diocese of	05	01	2-6
			11	08	465-469
Herefordshire		surnames	12	01	3-6
	Hereford	photographers	20	04	187-189
	Kingsland		12	01	3-6

county/region/city	town/parish		vol	no	pages
Herefordshire (cont.)	Woolhope	parish magazines	16	08	457-466
Hertfordshire		19th c crafts and trades	28	03	145-158
		County Council	23	01	31-39
		landscape strategies	13	08	456-467
		local councillors	19	04	159-161
		straw-plaiting	19	03	107-113
	Berkhamsted	friendly societies in	29	02	91-101
	Breachwood	plaiting trade	19	03	107-113
	Buntingford	medieval market town	29	04	194-211
	Hatfield	publishing history	05	03	81-84
	Hitchin	councillors	19	04	159-161
		history of	07	01	28-32
	Knebworth	publishing history	01	10	305-308
	Much Hadham	trades and crafts	28	03	145-158
	Rothamsted	agricultural research sta	23	02	85-91
		field names	02	12	353-356
	Royston	medieval market town	29	04	194-211
	St Paul's Walden	trades and crafts	28	03	145-158
	Stevenage	early conservation	24	03	153-163
	Tewin	19th century landscape	03	07	292-298
	Walkern	rural sanitation	21	04	156-161
	Westmill	account book	13	07	397-405
Huntingdonshire	Huntingdon	navigation to	26	02	102-114
	Swineshead	protestation returns	14	03	134-141
	Woolley	inventory of church goods	07	07	219-222
Ireland		early carved stones	04	04	140-142
		migration from	29	02	66-75
		military history 1590s	26	03	130-141
		travellers' tours	03	02	63-66
		vagrants from	21	02	66-69
Ireland, Northern		data sources	18	03	136-141
		historical exhibition	02	06	168-171
		local history in	12	03-04	167-168
	Belfast	historical exhibitions	02	06	168-171
	Lisburn	data sources	18	03	136-141
Isle of Man		local history in	22	02	74-83
		rope-making	10	07	332-333
Kent		gavelkind inheritance in	26	01	16-35
		land ownership in	05	03	66-71
		local history committee	11	04	225-228
		tithe surveys	12	02	88-92
	Aylesford	parish library	15	07	406-413
	Bexley	local politics	11	05	285-289
	Bromley	charity schools	24	03	145-152
	Greenwich	local history exhibition	03	01	39-42
	Hawkhurst	photographs of	02	02	41-43
	Lydd		23	03	163-169
	Maidstone	role of town	11	05	263-277
	Margate	visitor numbers	23	04	205-216
	Rainham	middle-class yeomen	26	01	16-35
	Romney Marsh	tithe surveys	12	02	88-92
	Sevenoaks	black community	19	01	8-15

county/region/city	town/parish		vol	no	pages
Kent *(cont.)*	Trottersclffe	19th century landscape	03	07	292-298
	West Wickham	in Civil War	22	03	138-143
Lake District		reservoir construction	26	03	155-167
		tourism in 1920s	24	04	217-224
		visitor numbers	23	04	205-216
Lancashire		antiquarians 19th c	26	01	3-14
		coalfields	18	01	5-12
		cricket in	25	02	95-108
		folk music 19th c	12	01	13-17
		music hall 19th c	09	08	379-386
		newspaper history	16	08	479-482
		probate inventories	04	04	157-161
			04	05	186-195
			04	08	320-324
		religious returns 1829	17	08	483-489
		trade directories	13	04	205-209
	Barrow-in-Furness	newspaper reports	11	06	321-326
	Belmont	industrial housing	23	03	146-154
	Blackburn	housing	15	01	6-20
	Blackpool	development late 19th c	24	04	194-205
		Tower	24	04	194-205
		visitor numbers 1921	23	04	205-216
		visitors to	13	06	323-331
	Bolton	cricket	25	02	95-108
	Chorley	recruitment WW1	17	04	243
	Furness	communities and society	26	01	36-47
	Fylde	hearth tax and settlement	11	07	385-389
		parishes and townships	27	01	3-17
	Horwich	industrial housing	23	03	146-154
	Lancaster	Georgian stonemasons	21	02	60-65
		water supplies	26	03	155-167
	Leyland	church	05	04	107-110
	Liverpool	archives	22	02	74-83
		local history in schools	12	08	403-407
		photographers	18	04	190-191
		poverty and poor	08	03	98-106
	Manchester	19th c cultural history	26	01	3-14
		census anomalies	13	08	481-487
		Chetham's Library	20	01	31-36
		John Rylands Library	19	02	71-73
		libraries	02	07	202-206
		literacy 16th/17th c	11	01	14-17
		women's suffrage	11	02	77-79
	Prescot	parish and townships	27	01	3-17
		Welsh community	26	04	223-236
	Preston	census analysis	11	03	155-161
	Silverdale	water supplies	26	03	155-167
	Ulverston		26	01	36-47
	Warrington	fire insurance records	17	03	141-149
Leeds		education archives	21	04	162-167
		libraries and archives	19	04	170-173
		museums	04	06	242-244

county/region/city	town/parish		vol	no	pages
Leicester		Edwardian poor	21	03	109-119
		Indian community 1965-95	28	04	225-241
		pawnbroking	20	01	24-30
		poor law apprenticeships	19	02	51-55
		Poor Law Union	19	02	51-55
Leicestershire		church briefs	15	06	345-354
	Ashby-de-la-Zouch	trade directories	11	02	85-88
	Hinckley	census 1831	14	02	79-90
		data sources	18	03	136-141
	Leicester	Edwardian poor	21	03	109-119
		Indian community 1965-95	28	04	225-241
		pawnbroking	20	01	24-30
		poor law apprenticeships	19	02	51-55
		Poor Law Union	19	02	51-55
	Lutterworth	census 1831	14	02	79-90
	Melton Mowbray	census 1831	14	02	79-90
		role of town	11	05	263-277
Lincolnshire		archives of	06	05	157-162
		county history project	09	03	111-114
		religious census 1851	11	07	375-381
		rural settlement	18	02	69-75
		truce terms	11	08	441-444
	Boston	medieval trade	22	01	18-40
	Canwick	agricultural workforce	27	03	130-143
	Corby Glen	census analysis	12	02	93-101
	Kesteven	religious returns 1829	17	08	483-489
	Lincoln	cathedral sculpture	24	02	83-90
		typhoid epidemic 1905	14	03	142
	Stamford	navigation schemes	26	02	102-114
	Timberland		06	05	157-162
Liverpool		archives	22	02	74-83
		local history in schools	12	08	403-407
		photographers	18	04	190-191
		poverty and poor	08	03	98-106
London		directories as source	18	04	187-189
		nurse children	19	03	100-106
		plans of	05	08	251-259
		voting charities	21	04	147-154
	Battersea	town meetings	27	03	163-182
	Chelsea	photographers	18	03	142-144
	Dulwich	public baths	25	03	142-152
	Lewisham	local history exhibition	03	01	39-42
	St. Dunstan	puritan wills	16	40	213-216
	Southwark	Shakespeare connections	07	02	42-46
Manchester		19th c cultural history	26	01	3-14
		census anomalies	13	08	481-487
		Chetham's Library	20	01	31-36
		John Rylands Library	19	02	71-73
		libraries	02	07	202-206
		literacy 16th/17th c	11	01	14-17
		women's suffrage	11	02	77-79
Middlesex		Anglo-Saxon charters	17	02	71-77

INDEX OF PLACES

county/region/city	town/parish		vol	no	pages
Middlesex *(cont.)*		suburban hedgerows	18	02	65-68
		Victoria County History	23	03	155-162
	Brent	hedgerows	18	02	65-68
	Chelsea	photographers	18	03	142-144
	Hammersmith & Fulham	Irish in	29	02	66-75
	Hampton-on-Thames	publishing history	03	05	183-184
	Hanwell	poor relief in	25	03	164-177
	Harrow	local history publishing	10	08	401-403
	Hendon	early censuses	18	01	19-20
		photographers	18	02	80-81
	Pinner	change in 19th c	17	04	199-204
	St. Dunstan	puritan wills	16	40	213-216
	Shepperton	clergy in	01	02	59-61
	West Ham	sources 20th c	20	03	109-117
Monmouthshire	Caldicot	electoral registers	11	01	30-34
	Chepstow	publishing history	02	07	212-214
Norfolk		Civil War	26	04	194-208
		deserted villages	13	08	471-474
		private law enforcement	14	04	226-232
	Aylsham	friendly societies in	29	02	91-101
	Holkham	farm buildings	12	08	407-420
	Kings Lynn	archaeological survey	08	04	139-145
	Kings Lynn	taxation 18th c	28	02	66-77
	Mattishall	church music	06	02	48-54
	Thetford	late medieval economy	29	04	194-211
Northamptonshire		illustrations of	05	05	151-154
		libraries	19	04	167-169
	Kettering	grammar school	15	03	137-143
	Peterborough	auction catalogues	13	03	131-139
	Pytchley	Domesday evidence	01	09	261-264
	Shutlanger	enclosures	01	06	178-181
	Stoke Bruerne	Domesday evidence	01	11	344-347
Northumberland		agriculture in	12	03-04	139-145
		local history societies	26	04	209-222
		photographs discussed	13	01	22-36
		war memorials	26	04	209-222
	Corbridge	folk memories	09	06	300-303
	Glendale	agriculture	12	03-04	139-145
Nottinghamshire		heraldic achievements	06	05	169-170
		Luddites in	28	01	24-35
	Bingham	clergy influence 18th c	15	07	388-401
	Laxton	social analysis	16	08	451-456
	Newark	clergy influence 18th c	15	07	388-401
	Nottingham	archives	22	02	74-83
		congregation at St Mary's	17	01	45
		street-lighting	11	06	327-330
	Styrrup	Methodist chapel	15	01	41-43
	Walkeringham	religious disputes	15	07	388-401
Oxfordshire		directories 18th c	17	06	343-350
		local history in	14	03	131-133
		militia	13	08	475-481

county/region/city	town/parish		vol	no	pages
Oxfordshire *(cont.)*		timber trades	20	02	73-79
	Banbury	militia	13	08	475-481
		role of town	11	05	263-277
	Blenheim	park	09	02	82-88
	Chinnor	photographers	19	02	74-76
	Culham	training college	12	03-04	161-166
	Middleton Stoney	churchyard survey	13	03	149-159
	Oxford	architecture 1699	26	02	102-114
		diocese of	25	01	7-16
		Merton College	28	01	16-23
		newspapers	10	06	271-276
Romney Marsh		tithe surveys	12	02	88-92
Rutland	Lyndon	weather records	15	02	70-72
Scotland		archive services	14	02	98-100
		archives	11	03	123-129
		archives 17th c	15	08	456-463
		commissary courts	17	01	4-10
		early carved stones	04	04	140-142
		education history	17	01	11-18
		enclosure records	07	08	265-274
		estate maps	12	01	26-30
		Fascism in	27	02	106-117
		General Registers of Poor	17	01	19-29
		graveyard memorials	23	02	66-84
		illegitimacy in	17	01	19-29
		industrial archaeology	12	06	296-303
		kirk session registers	11	04	229-233
		local history	09	07	353-356
			11	07	382-384
		local history sources	11	03	123-129
		maps and plans	12	06	296-303
		migration of labourers	14	01	35-43
		poor law in	17	01	19-29
		religious census 1851	27	04	194-217
		resort development	24	04	206-216
		sherriffs	03	08	329-331
		tourism in First World War	29	04	240-255
		travellers' tours	03	02	63-66
	Aberdeen	photographers	19	03	124-126
	Aberdeenshire	schools	14	08	471-476
	Aberdour	development as resort	24	04	206-216
	Angus	rural settlement	15	08	456-463
	Edinburgh		24	01	4-14
		archive repositories	09	07	353-356
		Scottish archives	01	12	374-377
	Falkirk	census statistics	10	05	259-264
	Glasgow	anti-Semitism	27	02	106-117
		migration to	18	03	127-135
	Jedburgh	education records	17	01	11-18
	Leadhills	mining and smelting	24	03	130-138
		miners' strike 1836	17	02	101-106
		village library	19	02	58-62

county/region/city	town/parish		vol	no	pages
Scotland (*cont.*)	New Lanark		06	04	118-120
	North Berwick	resort development	24	04	206-216
	Perthshire	bankruptcy sequestration	24	01	4-14
		migration to	17	01	19-29
	Peterhead	seaside resort	24	04	206-216
	Portobello	seaside resort	24	04	206-216
	Stirling	garden suburb	17	01	31-38
Sheffield		archives	22	02	74-83
		cutlery trades	25	04	194-208
		east end in 19th c	29	04	223-230
		steelmakers	13	06	349-352
Shropshire		archives	26	03	168-174
		Poor Law, Old	14	01	11-17
	Aldenham Park	iron forges	09	02	85-88
	Attingham	iron forges	09	02	85-88
	Bridgnorth	fairs	17	02	85-100
	Coalbrookdale	industrial history	02	08	225-229
	Heath	chapel	21	01	4-10
	Ironbridge	museums	09	06	289-93
	Shrewsbury		26	03	168-174
	Severn Gorge parishes	probate records	17	02	85-100
	Telford	probate records	17	02	85-100
	Wellington	evangelism in	10	03	116-124
Somerset		coalfield	18	01	5-12
	Angersleigh	footpaths	01	03	73-77
		Chapel Allerton	16	01	15-20
	Glastonbury Abbey	estate management	06	04	115-117
	Pitminster	footpaths	01	03	73-77
	Wedmore	medical care 18th c	20	04	173-186
		paupers	16	01	15-20
	Weston-super-Mare	Victorian parks	20	04	158-165
Staffordshire		local history teaching	13	05	290-296
		pottery industry	08	02	54-60
	Cannock	field books	15	02	67-69
	Colwich	route village	19	04	162-166
	Leek	silk industry	12	03-04	152-156
	Lichfield and Coventry	diocese of	15	06	355-357
	Penkhull	garden village	27	01	30-47
	Stafford	William Salt Library	19	03	114-116
	Stoke-on-Trent	garden villages	27	01	30-47
	Uttoxeter	in 17th c	20	03	128-136
	Walsall	cinemas	20	03	118-122
	West Bromwich	industrialisation	18	03	119-126
	Wolverhampton	cinemas	20	03	118-122
		crime 19th c	14	08	454-459
		retailing 1800-1950	29	03	167-182
	Yoxall	literacy	21	01	16-19
Suffolk		field names	17	05	285-289
		housing statistics	18	03	106-111
		rural unrest in	03	02	49-54
	Beccles	market trade	21	02	76-78
	Brandon	medieval market town	29	04	194-211

county/region/city	town/parish		vol	no	pages
Suffolk *(cont.)*	Bury St Edmunds	hustings 1868	14	06	359
	Coney Weston		16	01	21-23
	Flixton	charity	15	04	225-226
	Hawstead	tithe map	14	05	262-269
	Ipswich	Ragged School	14	01	34
	Newmarket	medieval market town	29	04	194-211
Surrey		Anglo-Saxon charters	17	02	71-77
		apprenticeships	08	07	232-236
		engravings and prints	10	07	355-360
	Caterham	conservation in	11	07	400-405
	Coulsdon	history exhibition	10	04	167-170
	Croydon	school records	17	08	490-493
	Nutfield	manorial	18	01	16-18
	Putney	chancery papers	17	07	408-416
		Royal Hospital and Home	24	01	15-26
	Richmond	Victorian vagrancy	21	02	66-69
Sussex		enclosure land sales	12	07	337-341
		housing statistics	18	03	106-111
		local history in	12	06	267-273
	Chichester	property research	13	01	11-14
	Oving		16	01	4-14
	Shoreham		03	08	319-324
	West Dean	historic landscapes	13	08	456-467
		parish boundaries	15	01	34-40
	Willingdon	grocery shop	09	03	126-129
Swaledale		lead-mining	18	03	112-118
Teesside		Chartists	18	02	76-79
Tyneside		Muslims in early 20th c	27	04	225-244
Wales		agricultural history	07	05	154-160
		agriculture 19th c	09	04	178-183
		archives	08	01	22-27
		archive services	13	06	341-345
			13	07	425-430
			13	08	468-471
		bibliography	09	01	16-22
		bibliography (medieval)	17	05	264-268
		bibliography since 1536	17	06	358-365
		demography	10	06	291-294
		early car owners	17	06	351-357
		enclosure records	07	08	265-274
		game laws in NE	26	03	142-154
		landscape history in	25	02	109-115
		local history in	09	01	16-22
		local history societies	10	08	404-411
		migration to Middlesbrough	12	02	74-79
		migration to Yorkshire	26	04	223-236
		public health records	14	04	202-210
		Rebecca Riots	08	07	255-257
		religious census 1851	27	04	194-217
		surnames	17	07	405-407
		topography 1770-1870	11	01	7-13
		travellers' tours	03	02	63-66

INDEX OF PLACES

county/region/city	town/parish		vol	no	pages
Wales *(cont.)*		valentine cards 19th c	09	03	134-141
		Victorian furniture	18	04	168-173
	Denbighshire	game laws 19th c	26	03	142-154
	Flintshire	game laws 19th c	26	03	142-154
	Merthyr Tydfil (Glams)	traditional housing	18	04	162-167
	Mostyn (Flints)	migration from	26	04	223-236
	St. Deiniol (Flints)	library	23	01	40-44
Warwickshire		ancient routeways	12	05	212-220
		moated sites	05	02	34-38
		new towns 19th c	10	04	186-195
		photography	20	04	166-172
	Arden, Forest of	fishponds	07	04	119-126
	Aston	development	10	04	186-195
	Baddesley Clinton	fishponds	07	04	119-126
	Birmingham	business communities	11	08	457-464
		demography 19th c	09	01	27-35
		local history in	02	09	274-275
		modern industries	16	03	146-150
		poor relief	16	01	25-31
		schools	29	02	102-113
		suburban development	15	05	259-271
	Bishopton	new town 19th c	10	04	186-195
	Compton Verney	iron forges	09	02	85-88
	Coventry	craft guilds	09	06	267-274
	Edgbaston	suburban development	15	05	259-271
	Hillfields	new town 19th c	10	04	186-195
	Ilmington	oral history	09	07	338-343
	Leamington Spa	development	10	04	186-195
	Stratford upon Avon		07	02	42-46
		new town 19th c	10	04	186-195
	Warwick	church monuments	03	05	217-219
		church rebuilding 1699	26	02	102-114
		conference report	26	03	175-177
Wash, The			03	04	153-159
Westmorland	Kendal	church brass	10	07	340-343
	Windermere	development in 1920s	24	04	217-24
Wiltshire		medieval land use	24	02	66-82
		tithings	27	01	3-17
	Salisbury	diocese of	11	08	465-469
Worcestershire		ancient routeways	12	05	212-220
		early charters	13	04	209-216
		wartime agriculture	29	02	76-90
	Dudley	photographic survey	09	05	222-225
	Powick	family reconstitution	09	01	9-15
	Ripple	Old Poor Law	12	03-04	136-139
Yorkshire		building plans	19	01	3-7
		Civil war in	02	09	261-264
		enclosure	29	01	14-24
		folk-names [rushes]	11	02	63-67
		memoranda rolls	05	08	242-246
		parsonage houses	08	02	47-53
		private law enforcement	14	04	226-232

county/region/city	town/parish		vol	no	pages
Yorkshire *(cont.)*		surnames	10	01	3-7
			10	04	171-177
			27	04	i-xx
		woodland history	16	02	73-82
	Barden estate	landscape history	26	02	66-79
	Barnsley	Welsh community	26	04	223-236
	Bolton Abbey	estate management	26	02	66-79
	Bolton Priory	monastic estate	26	02	66-79
	Bradfield	surname Ramscar	10	05	227-233
	Bradford	beerhouses	17	08	457-464
		coal-mining	23	04	188-198
	Calder valley	local history publishing	22	02	58-67
	Calverley cum Farsley		27	02	78-90
	Croft	parish church	21	03	120-125
	Elsecar	colliery	14	03	156-163
	Halifax	coal-mining	23	04	188-198
	Hallamshire	cutlers' apprentices	25	04	194-208
	Hallamshire	population mobility	27	04	i-xx
	Hebden Bridge	local history group	22	02	58-67
	Huddersfield	coal-mining	23	04	188-198
	Hull	trade directories	15	03	144-146
	Kilnhurst	potteries	24	01	37-43
	Leeds	education archives	21	04	162-167
		libraries and archives	19	04	170-173
		museums	04	06	242-244
	Low Wood	colliery	14	03	156-163
	Middlesbrough	immigration 19th c	12	02	74-79
	Nidd	village destruction	28	04	208-216
	Ouse, river	navigation projects	26	02	102-114
	Pocklington	enclosure	25	02	77-87
	Ramsker	surname derivation	10	05	227-233
	Rotherham	cannon-making	17	04	236-241
	Saddleworth	early woollen industry	15	05	277-287
	Sheffield	archives	22	02	74-83
		cutlery trades	25	04	194-208
		east end in 19th c	29	04	223-230
		steelmakers	13	06	349-352
	Slaidburn	encroachments on waste	11	03	141-147
		Stamford Bridge	04	02	84-85
	Stokesley	parish library	15	07	406-413
	Swaledale	lead-mining	18	03	112-118
	Tankersley	woodland	16	02	73-82
	Wakefield	deed registry	15	05	277-287
	York	York Museum	03	05	197-207
		navigation schemes	26	02	102-114

country/continent		vol	no	pages

2. Rest of the World

country/continent		vol	no	pages
Antarctica	exploration in	08	05	160-166
Austria	local history	11	04	207-217
Canada	Stanstead (Quebec)	04	01	9-11
Czechoslovakia	local history in	05	08	247-250
	Protestant history	05	02	51-55
Denmark	local history in	05	07	221-224
Ethiopia	local names and	14	08	468-469
Europe	local history in	21	03	99-108
	Protestant museums	05	02	51-55
Finland	local history	12	03-04	149-151
France	peasant revolts in	11	04	188-199
India	family history and	01	04	117-122
Italy	local history in	11	05	251-262
Japan	local history in	06	03	79-85
Norway	agricultural history	15	03	147-154
	local history in	06	08	262-265
		11	04	217-224
St Helena	local history of	28	02	108-122
Spain	local history in	24	02	91-101
Sweden	Skansen folk museum	03	05	197-207
United States of America	local history in	19	01	21-26
	local history education	15	04	204-211
	local history research	14	01	4-10

INDEX OF PEOPLE AND FAMILIES

This section of the index lists all individuals or families who have been the subject of a specific article or who have been referred to in some detail as case-studies or extended examples within thematic articles. It is not intended to be an exhaustive personal name index for the journal. *The Local Historian* has had comparatively few biographical articles, and it will be noted that a considerable proportion of the entries in this list in fact relate to family names which have been used as case-studies in work on surnames.

family name		*vol*	*no*	*pages*
Adshead	surname distribution	27	04	i-xx
Alchin	surname distribution	27	04	i-xx
Arkwright, Sir Richard		09	04	183-189
Ashburner, Margaret	diary	09	06	294-299
Ashurst	surname distribution	27	04	i-xx
Austen, Edward		28	04	217-224
Aylott	surname distribution	27	04	i-xx
Bailey, John Eglinton		26	01	3-14
Bale, Stewart		18	04	190-191
Barber, James		18	02	80-81
Barker, Thomas		15	02	70-72
Beauchamp family		03	05	217-219
Beavan, Rev. Thomas		16	08	457-466
Bedding, William		23	04	218-227
Bede, Venerable		02	04	102-105
Bell, Isaac		17	03	163-168
Biscoe, John		08	05	160-166
Bishop, William		15	06	358-360
Blundell, Nicholas	diary	09	06	294-299
Bottle family		20	02	65-72
Boyd, Percival	marriage index	22	02	68-73
Bradlaugh, Charles		08	06	221-227
Bray, Dr. Thomas		15	07	406-413
Bridgeman, Charles	inventory of projects	06	03	91-96
Brown, 'Capability'		03	08	332-349
	Sherborne Castle	25	04	231-241
Browne, John		15	04	225-226
Bunyan	surname distribution	27	04	i-xx
Bustin family		20	04	187-189
Byram, John	farm notebooks	13	05	270-276
Carus-Wilson, E.M.		22	01	18-40
Chambers, J.D.		09	07	323-333
Chetham, Humphrey		20	01	31-36
Cleet, James Henry		19	04	174-176
Coke, Thomas		09	07	323-333
Coleman, O.		22	01	18-40
Cox, Barrie	place name interpretation	22	03	114-127

family name		vol	no	pages
Culley, George		12	03-04	139-145
Cussans, John Edwin		03	06	253-256
d' Ewes family		22	01	41-42
Dale, David		06	04	118-120
Defoe, Daniel		10	01	27-32
Devonshire	dukes of	26	02	66-79
Dickens, Charles	as social commentator	08	07	243-250
Digby family		25	04	231-241
Dolley, R.H.M.		25	01	3-6
Dunn, Matthias		16	07	418-424
Dyos, H.J.		11	05	278-284
Earwaker, John Parson		26	01	3-14
Edwards, Thomas Ambrose		01	11	325-330
Eliot, George	as social commentator	08	07	243-250
Emmison, F.G.	obituary	26	02	115-116
Ernle, Lord		09	07	323-333
Errington, Rev. John		15	07	388-401
Fell, Sarah	account books	26	01	36-47
Fiennes, Celia		10	01	27-32
Finberg, H.P.R		06	02	38-44
	obituary	11	05	306-307
		14	07	392-399
		21	03	99-108
		29	04	256-262
Fitzhugh, Terrick		22	01	6-13
Fitzwilliam family		16	02	73-82
		24	01	37-43
Flagg, Amy		19	04	174-176
Fleming, William	commonplace books	26	01	36-47
Foster, Canon W.C.		06	05	157-62
Fremantle, Sir Thomas		11	03	134-141
Fuller	surname distribution	16	07	392-404
Gaskell, Elizabeth	as social commentator	09	02	75-79
George III		29	04	212-222
Gibson family		25	03	153-163
Gilbert, Sir Henry		23	02	85-91
Giuseppi, M.S.		06	02	45-48
Gladstone, W.E.		23	01	40-44
Graham, James		21	04	162-167
Green, William		17	04	212-219
Greengrass	surname distribution	27	04	i-xx
Harrison, William Jerome		20	04	166-172
Hedderley, James		18	03	142-144
Hill, William		19	02	74-76
Hine, Reginald Leslie		07	01	28-32
Hooper, Max		14	01	28-33
Hoskins, W.G.		06	02	38-44
		14	04	195-201
		14	07	392-399
		21	03	99-108
	obituary/appreciation	22	01	14-17
		22	03	144-146
		22	04	170-183

family name		vol	no	pages
Hoskins, W.G. *(cont.)*		29	04	256-262
Howard, Ebenezer		27	01	30-47
Howard, Sir John		04	07	300-301
		05	01	7-8
Hughes, Lewis		01	02	59-61
Hutton, William		04	06	251-254
Jackson, Reverend Edward	diaries	26	01	36-47
John, King	lost treasure of	03	04	153-159
Keeler	surname distribution	27	04	i-xx
Kerridge, Eric	agricultural historian	09	07	323-333
Kip, Johannes	inventory of engravings	04	01	23-25
Law, Rev. Frederick Henry		21	03	120-125
Lawes, Sir John		23	02	85-91
Leaver family		20	02	65-72
Lennard, Sir Stephen		22	03	138-143
Lewin, Rev. Edmund		13	07	397-405
Luggar/ Lugger family		12	01	3-6
Lumley-Saville family		23	04	188-198
MacKenzie, Murdo		18	03	127-135
Malleson, Elizabeth		20	04	155-157
Marshall, J.D.		06	02	38-44
		06	06	182-185
		07	04	102-108
		14	06	325-331
		29	04	256-262
Mell family		16	06	343-345
		17	07	391-395
Meverill, Sir Sampson		15	07	388-401
Midgley, L. Margaret	obituary	22	04	209-212
Napier, Sir Robert	names from	14	08	468-469
Nichols, Mary	diary	25	03	130-141
North, Lord Roger		26	03	130-141
O'Neil, John	diary	09	06	294-299
Ogilby, John		01	12	357-360
Ogilby, John		07	06	196-208
Overton, John		10	03	139-141
Owen, Robert		06	04	118-120
Paine, Thomas		08	06	221-227
Palliser	surname distribution	27	04	i-xx
Paris, Matthew		02	04	102-105
Parker, Rowland		12	08	391-394
Patten family	Sheffield cutlers	25	04	194-208
Petre, Robert 9th Lord		29	04	212-222
Pevsner, Sir Nikolaus	obituary	15	08	454-455
Phythian Adams, Charles		21	03	99-108
		26	01	36-47
		29	04	256-262
Pitt, William		14	06	348-351
Pitt-Rivers, General		02	05	141-144
Princes in the Tower		04	07	300-301
		05	01	7-8
Rain, John		17	07	417-422
Ramsbottom	surname distribution	27	04	i-xx

family name		vol	no	pages
Ramsden, Sir John		23	04	188-198
Ramsker	surname origins	10	05	227-233
Rawlinson, Richard		02	05	130-133
Rebow, Mary		29	04	212-222
Reed, Andrew		24	01	15-26
Repton, Humphrey	inventory of projects	03	08	332-349
Richard III		04	07	300-301
		05	01	7-8
Riggs	surname distribution	27	04	i-xx
Roberts, Catherine		19	02	51-55
Robinson families		09	01	23-25
Robson	surname distribution	27	04	i-xx
Rothwell	surname distribution	27	04	i-xx
Round	surname distribution	27	04	i-xx
Russo, David J.		19	01	21-26
Saxton, Christopher		01	12	357-360
Shakespeare, William		07	02	42-46
Sharp, Cecil		09	07	343-347
Shrewsbury, earls of		15	07	388-401
Smith	surname distribution	16	07	392-404
Speed, John		01	12	357-360
		07	06	196-208
Spufford family		05	06	173-176
Stenton, Sir Frank		25	01	3-6
Surbey, Thomas		26	02	102-114
Tawney, R.H.		22	02	58-67
Telford, Thomas		02	08	225-229
Thurston, Frederick		19	01	27-29
Titterton family		20	01	3-8
Tucker	surname distribution	16	07	392-404
Ullathorne	surname distribution	27	04	i-xx
Walker	surname distribution	16	07	392-404
Walker family	ironfounders	17	04	236-241
Wall, Aaron		16	01	15-20
Waller, William Chapman		24	04	229-242
Walter, Lucy		05	05	141-144
Warham, Thomas		20	01	37-39
Warwick, earls of		03	05	217-219
Waylett, William		23	03	163-169
Wedgwood family		08	03	78-85
Wesley, Charles		03	04	143-149
Westover, John		20	04	173-186
Wharton, Duke of	lead interests	18	03	112-118
Wheeler	surname distribution	16	07	392-404
Whitelock, Dorothy		25	01	3-6
William of Worcester		03	01	1-8
Williamson, G.C.	trade tokens	06	02	55-61
Willis family		07	04	112-118
Wilson, George Washington		19	03	124-126
Winchester, Angus J.L.		29	04	256-262
Woods, Katherine		16	01	4-14
Yallop, William	market accounts	21	02	76-78

INDEX OF AUTHORS

author	vol	no	pages
Adams, I.H	12	01	26-30
Airs, Malcolm	15	08	454-455
Aitken, C.Peter	17	01	31-38
Alban, John R.	14	05	284-288
Aldred, Margaret G.	04	05	198-201
Aldsworth, F.G.	15	01	34-40
Alexander, Andrew	29	03	167-182
Alvey, Norman G.	21	04	147-155
	24	01	15-27
Ambler, R. W.	10	02	59-64
	11	07	375-381
	17	08	483-489
Amos, Joanne	28	04	208-216
Anderson, Sheila	20	02	88-89
Ashby, M.K.	10	07	327-332
Ashmore, Owen	04	04	157-161
	04	05	186-195
Ashworth, G.J.	08	07	232-236
Aspinall, Peter J.	11	06	343-349
Aston, Michael	15	06	323-332
Atkins, P.J.	10	03	135-138
	18	04	187-189
Austin, Tony	16	05	282-283
Bagley, J.J.	04	06	227-231
	04	08	320-324
Bailey, Keith	17	02	71-77
Bailey, Mark	29	04	194-211
Bailey, Patrick	04	01	9-11
Baird, Kenneth D.	03	03	112-114
	03	08	329-331
	04	04	140-142
Baker, Alan R.H.	05	03	66-71
Baker, Frank	03	04	143-149
Baker, Timothy	23	03	155-162
Banister, J.N.	05	04	107-110
Banks, F.R.	04	06	251-254
Barke, Michael	10	05	259-264
Barker, Rosalin	14	06	332-340
	15	08	486-489
Barker, T.C.	01	05	140-145
Barnes, Bernard	15	05	277-287
Barney, John M.	28	02	66-77
Barnsley, John H.	16	03	146-150
Bartle, G.F.	16	04	204-206
Batley, J.C.	07	06	214-216
Batley, James	10	04	167-170
	10	07	353-360
	11	07	400-405
	12	07	360-364
	12	08	421-429
	13	03	159-167
	13	04	224-232
Battagel, Arthur	15	03	147-154
Beadle, Shane	18	01	5-12
Beaumont, Heather	26	02	66-79
Beck, Joan	02	06	165-167
Beckett, Ian F.W.	13	08	475-481
	16	07	405-411
Beckett, J.V.	12	01	7-12
	16	08	451-456
	29	01	14-24
Beckley, Susan	12	03-04	158-60
Beckwith, Ian	11	08	441-444
	14	04	232-233
Bellamy, Joyce			
Bellingham, Roger A.	25	02	77-87
Benjamin, E. Alwyn	17	07	405-407
Bennett, Martyn	22	04	191-202
Bennison, Brian	25	01	31-42
Benson, John	17	04	226-235
	29	03	167-182
Bensusan, Arnold E.	01	10	293-296
	05	03	77-79
Beresford, Maurice W.	03	07	271-278
	03	08	325-328
	04	03	101-109
	05	08	260-269
Bertelli, Sergio	11	05	251-262
Bettey, J.H.	11	03	129-133
	12	05	228-234
	14	02	93-97
	28	01	3-15
Bigmore, P.G.	08	08	282-287
Bird, Polly	25	03	142-153
Bisceglia, Louis	14	01	4-10
Black, Jeremy	23	02	103-110
Blackwood, R.G.	26	04	194-208
Blake, Robert et al	13	08	451-456
Blakeney, T.S.	04	07	300-301
Bland, D.S.	05	03	72-76
Bloxham, R.N.	07	05	161-165
Blyth, Joan E.	12	08	403-407
Bond, James	18	02	53-57
Bond, Maurice	04	06	219-226
	04	07	267-274

author	vol	no	pages	author	vol	no	pages
Bond, Maurice *(cont.)*	04	08	307-314		29	01	3-13
	04	08	354-358		29	03	152-166
Bond, Shelagh M.	02	10	297-303	Clayton, Dorothy	19	02	71-73
Bonney, Margaret	22	01	18-40	Clinker, C.R.	01	03	90-94
Boston, Noel	06	02	48-54		02	09	257-260
Bouquet, Michael	05	06	177-182	Cole, E.J.L.	07	06	189-191
Bourgeois II, Eugene J.	26	03	130-141	Collins, Mildred	18	03	119-126
Bowden, Catherine	19	03	114-16	Collis, Ivor P.	02	12	368-372
Bracher, Terry	26	03	168-174	Colyer, R.J.	11	07	406-413
Bradfield, Hazel	16	04	213-216	Cookson, Gillian	19	01	3-7
Bratt, Clifford	03	03	126-129	Cooper, Elizabeth	10	08	401-403
Brett, Donald	16	07	392-404	Copinger, Hubert S.A	02	01	1-3
Brinkley, Richard	11	01	7-13	Coppock, J.T.	03	07	292-298
Brinkworth, E.R.C.	02	01	19-22		04	02	49-55
	02	02	50-53	Cossons, Arthur	05	02	39-43
	02	03	82-86	Cowan, Michael	26	03	175-177
Briscoe, A. Daly	11	08	465-469	Coward, Harold	09	08	394-398
Bromwich, David	18	01	23	Cowell, B.	29	01	14-24
Brooks, F.W.	10	08	385-389	Cowper, Julia M.	04	04	143-152
Brooks, Leslie	15	05	288-295	Cox, Benjamin G.	04	05	202-205
Brown, A.F.J.	03	02	49-54	Cox, Christopher	18	02	58-64
Brown, Janet	26	04	209-222	Cox, David C.	06	08	260-261
Brown, Richard	13	03	140-145	Cox, Jeff	16	03	133-145
Bruce, J.W.G.	04	04	162-164		16	04	217-227
Brumhead, Derek	28	04	194-207		16	08	467-477
Bryant, V.J.M.	10	04	183-185		17	02	85-100
Bryon, J.F.W.	08	06	205-211	Cox, Nancy	16	03	133-145
Bullock, Humphry	01	04	117-121		16	04	217-227
	01	07	205-208		16	08	467-477
Burgess, Frederick	06	07	229-233	Cox, Nancy	17	02	85-100
Cadell, Patrick	11	08	445-448	Cox, Ron	17	08	490-493
Camp, Anthony J.	22	02	68-73	Crackles, Eva	11	02	63-67
Carter, Paul	25	03	164-177	Crane, Eva	29	03	130-151
Casely-Hayford,				Crang, Alan	07	02	42-46
Augustus	20	02	59-64	Cressy, David	14	03	134-141
Catt, Jon	16	08	479-482	Crompton, Catherine A.	28	03	145-158
Chaloner, W.H.	04	08	315-319	Crosby, Alan G.	25	04	242-244
Chaplin, Robin	09	02	82-88	Crowe, Helen	20	02	80-83
	10	04	186-195	Crowley, J.M	07	05	161-165
	12	03-04	131-135	D'Cruze, Shani	17	03	158-162
	12	06	277-283	Daff, Trevor	09	06	275-279
	12	07	343-348	Dalton, Roger	28	01	36-49
	13	05	262-270	Daniels, Christopher	13	03	140-145
	14	04	211-221	Dare, Edwin H.	24	04	229-242
	14	07	419-427	David, Rob	21	03	126-130
	15	07	414-430	Davidson, Alan	09	06	283-289
Chapman, John ✓	12	07	337-341	Davidson, Thomas	03	06	237-248
Chase, Malcolm ✓	18	02	76-79	Davies, C. Stella	04	04	154-156
Chilton, C.W.	15	03	144-146	Davies, G.J.	11	07	395-399
Chiswell, Ann	16	03	156-160	Davies, John	17	05	264-268
Christie, Peter	15	02	80-84		17	06	358-365
Clark, Gillian	19	03	100-106	Davies, Stuart	12	05	235-240

author	vol	no	pages	author	vol	no	pages
Davis, Graham	14	05	276-281	Elton, G.R.	04	03	89-94
Dedman, M.J.	12	07	353-359	Emmison, F.G.	13	04	217-223
Digby, Anne	12	05	206-211		14	07	411-416
Dils, Joan	17	05	269-276	Emmony, David	24	02	83-90
Dobbie, J.L.	17	08	465-474	English, Barbara	16	07	388-391
Dodds, Klaus-John	21	04	168-176		19	03	117-119
Donnachie, Ian	12	06	296-303	Evans, Brian M.	07	05	154-160
Dopson, Laurence	01	03	73-76	Evans, Nesta	14	01	24-27
	01	12	374-377		15	04	225-226
	02	07	202-206		15	06	361
	03	04	150-152		21	02	76-78
Douch, John	23	03	163-169		22	04	203-207
Douch, Robert	03	07	286-91	Everett, B.G.	09	03	130-134
	06	07	218-222	Everitt, Alan	06	02	38-44
Doughan, David	23	02	92-97		08	04	118-125
Douglas, Elizabeth	03	02	66-69		08	06	196-204
Downey, Matthew T.	15	04	204-211		11	05	263-277
Downing, Ruth	17	05	285-295	Fairman, Tony	28	04	217-224
Druker, Janet	12	08	394-400	Farrant, John H.	12	06	267-273
Duckham, Baron F.	06	01	8-10	Farrant, Sue	12	03-04	136-139
	07	03	84-87	Farrell, Jerome	29	02	66-75
	08	08	272-281	Faull, Margaret L.	15	01	21-23
	15	06	338-344		15	08	483-485
	17	06	351-357	Fendick, Eustace A.	15	01	41-43
Duggan, Edward P.	11	08	457-465	Ferns, J.L.	17	04	236-241
Duman, Daniel H.	11	02	68-71	Field, Clive D.	27	04	194-217
Durie, Alastair J.	24	04	206-216	Field, John	13	07	388-396
	29	04	240-255		16	04	195-203
Durtnell, C.S	03	07	279-282		17	07	396-404
	04	02	56-61	Finch, Peter	18	01	16-18
Dyer, Alan	12	06	285-292	Fines, J.	06	08	254-259
	16	01	32-35	Fink, D.P.J.	01	08	230-233
Dyer, Christopher	16	05	260-265	Fisk, Audrey	29	02	91-101
Dymond, David P.	10	07	344-352	FitzHugh, Terrick	01	01	30-33
	22	01	41-42	Fladby, Rolf	06	08	262-266
Dyos, H.J.	03	05	191-197		11	04	217-224
	04	03	116-119	Fletcher, Allan	26	03	142-154
	04	07	275-281	Fletcher, John M.	28	01	16-23
Eaton, V.	01	06	182-185	Forbes, Heather	23	02	98-102
Ecclestone, Martin	19	02	63-70	Foster, David	11	07	385-389
Eden, Peter	07	02	53-59	Foulds, T.	16	08	451-456
Egan, David	13	06	341-345	Fowler, Simon	21	02	66-69
	13	07	425-430		27	03	144-162
	13	08	468-471	Franklin, T. Bedford	01	06	178-181
Elbourne, R.P.	12	01	13-17		01	09	261-267
Elliott, Bernard J.	13	02	74-78		01	10	297-300
	14	02	76-78		01	11	344-347
	14	03	143-148	Freeman, Mike	18	04	183-186
	15	08	474-477	French, E.C.W.	02	01	4-7
Elliott, Vivien	10	06	282-290		02	07	197-201
Ellison, Leslie	15	02	74-79	Fussell, G.E.	04	01	1-8
Elrington, Christopher	22	03	128-137		04	08	338-345

author	vol	no	pages	author	vol	no	pages
Fussell, G.E. *(cont.)*	15	03	157-160		02	09	265-267
Gant, R.L.	11	01	30-34		02	10	293-296
Gardner, E.M.	02	11	326-329		02	11	337-339
Garnett, R.G.	06	04	118-120	Hall, Ray	11	06	340-343
	09	04	163-171	Hall, William G.	16	01	15-20
Garrad, Larch S.	10	07	332-333	Hamilton-Edwards,			
Garside, Bernard	03	05	183-184	Gerald	01	11	325-330
Garside, Patricia L.	13	02	67-74	Hargreaves, John	13	07	416-424
Gaskell, S. Martin	10	02	65-69	Harley, J.B.	05	01	9-16
	16	01	4-14		05	05	130-140
Gathercole, P.W.	02	05	141-144		05	07	202-211
	02	05	145		05	08	251-259
Gay, Tim	14	05	282-283		07	06	196-208
Gelling, Margaret	01	02	51-55		07	07	223-231
	01	08	241-245		07	08	265-274
	01	11	340-343		08	02	61-71
	02	10	289-292		08	03	86-97
	03	01	9-12		08	05	167-179
	11	01	3-6	Harris, Alan	07	03	95-98
	12	06	273-277	Harris, P.V.	01	04	122-124
	13	04	209-216	Harrison, Barry	17	02	78-84
	22	03	114-127	Harrison, Brett	18	01	21-22
Gerhold, Dorian	17	07	408-416	Harrison, Brian	08	04	135-138
	17	08	475-482		08	05	180-186
Gibson, Jeremy S.W.	13	02	100-102	Harrison, Christopher J.	15	02	67-69
	14	04	222-225		20	03	126-127
	15	04	218-220	Hartley, W.C. Eyre	02	10	311-312
	17	05	281-284	Hartley, W.P.	23	04	188-198
Giles, Patricia	16	05	Supp.	Harvey, A.D.	13	06	332-338
Gill, Michael C.	18	03	112-118	Harvey, W.S.	17	02	101-106
Gillespie, W.H.	02	04	111-113		19	02	58-62
Gillett, E.	05	07	224-230		24	03	130-138
Gittings, Clare	21	02	51-59	Hassall, W.O.	02	05	130-133
Glaister, R.T.D.	17	01	11-18		02	08	245-246
Godfrey, Michael	06	06	192-197	Hastings, R. Paul	10	05	221-226
Gooder, Arthur	09	08	387-394		14	04	226-232
Gordon, Peter	10	06	277-281		15	07	406-413
Gorsky, Martin	25	01	17-30	Hayns, David	22	02	89-96
Grant, Betty	03	04	160-165	Hearl, Trevor	16	06	346-350
Grant, Jean M.	01	10	305-308	Heath, John	15	04	221-224
Green, Alan	03	05	208-212	Hector, L.C.	01	06	174-177
Green, E.R.R.	02	06	168-171		06	02	45-48
Green, Eric	24	03	145-152	Helen, Miles	04	01	26-27
Greet, Mike	17	03	163-168	Henderson, L.O.	04	06	232-234
Grey, Peter	10	02	70-75	Henstock, Adrian	14	02	68-75
Grigg, David	06	05	152-156		14	03	149-155
Gutchen, Robert M.	11	08	452-456		15	07	388-401
	16	02	93-99	Heron, Vanessa	08	06	213-217
Gwynne, Terence	12	02	74-79	Hey, David	27	04	i-xx
Hair, Paul E.H.	12	01	3-6	Heymer, Edward	02	02	41-43
	21	01	4-10	Hicks, F.W. Potto	01	07	220-224
Halcrow, Elizabeth M.	01	10	308-311		02	02	44-47

author	vol	no	pages	author	vol	no	pages
Higgs, Edward	19	02	56-57	Jagger, Peter J.	23	01	40-44
	22	04	184-190	James, Peter	20	04	166-172
Higgs, J.W.Y.	05	07	221-224	Jenkins, David	09	04	178-183
Hill, Christopher	01	01	13-17	Jenkins, Gareth	08	07	255-257
Hill, Julian	14	01	11-17		09	03	134-141
Hill, William G.	20	04	173-186	Jennings, Bernard	22	02	58-67
Hillier, Richard	13	03	131-139	Jennings, Paul	17	08	457-464
Hilton, Rodney H.	01	03	82-85	John, Angela V.	17	03	150-157
	01	03	86-89	Johnson, C.J.	14	01	28-33
	10	08	390-394	Johnson, L.C.	04	08	329-334
Historicus	02	08	238-244	Johnson, W. Branch	01	04	127-129
Hobsbawm, E.J.	03	03	95-101 *Article*		02	05	134-137
Hocart, Richard	21	01	20-25		03	06	253-256
Hodges-Paul, R.T.	03	07	299-300		04	03	98-100
	03	08	319-323		04	08	325-328
Hodson, Deborah	29	03	167-182		06	01	18-21
Hooke, Della	12	05	212-220		07	01	28-32
	27	01	18-29	Johnson, Wendy	13	04	195-204
Hoppé, E.O.	03	07	296-299	Johnston, G.D.	03	06	249-252
Horn, Pamela	11	03	134-141		04	02	67-72
	12	03-04	161-166	Johnston, J.A.	09	01	9-15
	13	06	353-359		15	08	478-482
	15	01	25-32	Jones, A.G.E.	08	05	160-165
Hoskins, W.G.	03	01	1-8	Jones, B.C.	02	03	76-79
Howard-Drake, Jack	25	01	7-16	Jones, G.E.	11	06	331-334
Howe, John R.	17	04	212-218	Jones, John	29	03	167-182
Howells, Brian	10	06	291-294	Jones, L.J.	15	03	155-156
	10	08	404-411	Jones, Magdalen	11	06	331-334
Hudson, Pat	25	04	209-222	Jones, Melvyn	14	03	156-163
Huggins, Mike	21	03	126-130		16	02	73-82
Hughes, Paul	26	02	102-114		26	04	223-236
Hume, Robert	15	06	355-357	Jones-Baker, Doris	23	01	4-19
Humphery-Smith				Kain, R.J.P.	12	02	88-92
Cecil R.	11	08	470-472	Keil, Ian	06	04	115-117
Hurst, J.G.	02	07	193-196	Kennerley, Eija	12	03-04	149-151
Husbands, Christopher	14	03	164-167	Kerridge, Eric	07	01	2-7
Hussey, Trevor	17	06	327-342	Ketchley, C.P	02	03	69-71
Hutton, Barbara	07	03	92-94		02	09	268-270
	12	02	81-84		02	10	309-311
	16	06	323-326		02	11	334-336
Hutton, Kenneth	05	03	81-84		02	12	357-361
	08	08	288-291		05	04	111-114
Ibbotson, E.M.H.	09	07	338-343	Kidd, Alan. J	26	01	3-15
Iley, Walter R.	09	06	300-303	Killingray, David	19	01	8-15
Iredale, David A.	06	05	163-165	King, Steve	27	02	78-90
	07	06	182-189	Kingsford, Peter	19	04	159-161
Isaac, Peter	24	02	102-111		23	01	31-39
Jackson, James C.	04	02	73-77	Kinnell, Margaret	17	04	219-225
	05	01	23-28	Kirby, David A.	11	01	24-29
Jackson, Stephen	16	05	266-277	Kirkman, Ken	15	08	464-467
Jackson, T.V.	17	03	141-149		17	04	199-204
Jacob, Kenneth A.	06	02	55-61	Kissock, Jonathan	24	02	66-82

author	vol	no	pages	author	vol	no	pages
Knightbridge, A.A.H.	07	07	219-222	Mackinnon, Ann Dolina	27	02	91-105
Knowlden, Patricia E.	22	03	138-143	MacMahon, K.A.	05	07	212-217
Komatsu, Y.	06	03	79-86	Maidbury, Lawrence	01	10	312-314
Kuhlicke, F.W.	05	04	98-106		01	12	368-371
Ladurie, Emmanuel Le R	11	04	188-199		02	01	15-18
					02	04	114-117
Lamb, V.B.	05	01	7-8		03	03	108-112
Langdo, A.J.	02	08	230-231	Maitles, Henry	27	02	106-116
Larkham, Peter J.	18	04	183-186	Mann, Richard I.	05	04	115-120
	19	03	120-123	Manson, Michael	25	02	66-76
Latham, R. E.	01	11	333-335	Marriott, John	20	03	109-117
	01	01	5-8	Marshall, J. D.	02	05	146-148
	01	02	47-50		03	05	185-189
	01	03	77-81		06	01	11-17
	01	04	112-116		06	07	233-234
	01	05	155-158		09	06	294-299
	01	11	331-333		12	08	403-407
Lavender, F.	02	06	181		13	01	3-11
Law, C.M	10	03	142-146		15	06	333-337
	10	01	13-26		22	01	14-17
Lawless, Richard J.	27	04	225-244		23	03	146-154
Lawrence, Martin	21	01	11-15		26	01	36-47
Lawton, Ann	16	08	457-466	Marshall, Rosalind	11	07	382-384
Le Hardy, W.	01	05	146-152	Mason, A. Stuart	29	04	194-211
Le Patourel, Jean	11	02	89-93	Matthews, A.G.	01	02	59-60
Leach, Terence R.	06	03	74-78	Matthews, M.H.	16	01	25-31
Leaver, Rex	20	02	65-72	Maynard, John	13	05	276-280
	29	01	25-42		14	07	407-410
Leech, C.E.	11	02	77-79	Mayne, L. Bruce	01	12	357-360
Legg, E.	06	03	86-90		03	01	20-31
Lello, John	11	08	473-476		03	02	63-66
Lever, R.J.A.W.	10	04	180-182		03	05	197-207
Lewin, J.	08	02	47-53	McClure, Peter	13	02	80-86
Lewis, Myrddin J.	17	05	277-280	McCord, Norman	12	01	31-36
Lewis, R.A.	13	05	290-296		13	01	23-35
Lindley, Philip	24	02	83-90	McCrone, David	25	04	223-230
Little, John E.	04	04	152-153	McCutcheon, E.	13	08	471-474
	04	05	195-197	McGloin, P.R.	13	06	323-331
Little, Reginald H.	07	04	112-118	McGuinness, Mary	06	07	235-242
Lloyd, E.R.	07	02	47-52	McInnes, Angus	20	03	128-136
Lloyd-Jones, Roger	17	05	277-280	McIntosh, K.H.	01	11	348-349
Lockett, Terence	08	02	54-60	McKay, D.A.	02	04	102-105
	08	03	78-85		02	06	176-180
Lockhart, D.G.	14	01	35-43		02	11	321-325
Lomas, Tim	18	04	174-182		03	03	105-107
Lowe, Roy	12	05	223-228		03	05	213-216
Loyn, H.R.	25	01	3-6	McKinley, R.A.	08	08	299-302
Lucas, Peter	11	06	321-326	McLaughlin, J.	18	02	65-68
Lynn, Pauline	28	03	159-175	McNiven, Peter	19	02	71-73
Maar, Grete	11	04	207-216	McPherson, Gayle	29	04	240-255
Macdonald, Stuart	12	03-04	139-145	Mellor, George R.	02	04	97-101
Mackerness, E.D.	11	06	315-320	Metcalf, Fay D.	15	04	204-211

author	vol	no	pages	author	vol	no	pages
Meyer, Harry	01	02	43-46		16	03	161-167
Meyer, W.R.	21	04	162-167	Needham, G.	10	07	340-343
Micklewright, F.H. A.	07	08	253-257	Neville, Graham	29	02	76-90
	08	06	221-227	Newall, B.J.	02	09	274-276
Miller, Stuart T.	15	08	468-473	Newby, Howard	10	07	334-339
	17	07	417-422	Newman, A.G.	13	05	280-289
Millman, Roger	13	08	456-467	Newton, K.C.	03	02	81-94
Mills, Dennis R.	06	08	271-278		07	03	88-91
	07	01	7-13	Noble, Margaret	15	02	86-92
	11	04	200-206	Northeast, Peter	06	07	223-224
	13	02	86-98	Nuttall, Derek	26	04	237-245
	18	02	69-75	O'Neill, Cliff	23	04	205-216
	24	04	225-228		24	04	217-224
	27	03	130-143	Owen, D. Huw	14	02	91-92
Mills, Joan	18	02	69-75		25	02	109-115
	27	03	130-143	Owen, Dorothy M.	05	02	44-50
Mitchell, Ian	14	06	348-351		07	01	17-27
Mitchison, Rosalind	11	04	229-234		08	07	237-242
Moorsom, Norman	06	07	225-227		09	02	65-74
Morgan, Gerald	25	03	178-185		16	03	151-155
Morgan, H.G.	11	03	162-166	Page, David	11	02	85-88
Morgan, J.B.	02	07	207-211	Page, Stephen J.	20	01	24-30
Morgan, Philip	17	01	39-44		21	03	109-119
Morgan, R.R.	13	01	11-14		23	01	20-30
Morgan, Raine	19	01	18-20	Paget, Mary	15	03	166-173
Moriarty, Catherine	20	03	123-125	Palliser, D.M.	15	03	155-156
Morris, G.M.	10	05	253-258		16	04	207-212
Morris, Pam	19	04	162-166	Pankhurs, Richard	14	08	468-469
Morris, R.J.	09	05	241-245	Parker, Rowland	12	08	391-394
Mortimer, R.S.	03	02	55-61	Parry, Bryn R.	08	01	22-27
Morton, A.L.	05	05	141-144	Parton, A.G.	08	02	47-53
Mosdell, Jack	09	03	126-129		16	01	25-31
Mottram, A.S.	08	04	139-145	Paul, E. Derryan	15	01	3-5
Muir, Augustus	06	04	128-133	Paul, Norman	23	03	130-145
Muir, Richard	28	04	208-216	Pemberton, Wilfred A.	13	07	397-405
Mumford, W.F.	09	04	175-177		15	06	345-354
	10	02	83-87	Pennethorne, Gwyneth	01	04	102-105
Munby, Lionel M.	02	01	8-11	Penny, Nell	18	01	19-20
	02	03	65-68	Percival, Arthur	15	05	272-276
	04	01	65-66	Percy-Smith, H.K.	01	03	70-72
	05	08	247-250	Perkyns, Audrey	26	01	16-35
	06	04	134-135	Perry, Peter	09	07	334-337
	07	03	78-83	Petree, J. Foster	04	06	245-250
	07	04	102-108	Pettifer, Ernest W.	03	06	231-236
	12	07	330-337	Petty, M.J.	14	08	460-467
	16	02	90-92	Phelps, P.J.	11	06	331-334
	21	03	120-125	Phillips, C.W.	05	06	166-172
	22	01	8-13	Phythian-Adams, Charles	09	06	267-274
Munro, John	19	04	167-169				
Munslow, F.W.	02	12	353-356		22	04	170-183
Musson, A.E.	01	09	273-276	Pickford, Chris	21	01	11-15
Neave, David	08	06	213-217	Pine, L.G.	01	06	166-168

author	vol	no	pages	author	vol	no	pages
Pine, L.G. *(cont.)*	01	08	238-240	Richardson, R.C.	11	01	14-17
	02	02	37-40	Riden, Philip	14	01	18-23
Pirie, Elizabeth	01	07	202-204	Ridge, C. Harold	01	01	18-22
Place, Robin	01	05	134-139	Rix, Michael M.	02	08	225-229
	01	12	378-381		05	02	56-60
	03	04	170-174	Roberts, Brian K.	05	02	34-38
Pocock, Michael H.	02	09	261-264		07	04	119-126
Pollard, Michael	09	07	343-347		09	05	233-241
Pollard, Sidney	04	05	177-181	Roberts, D.E.	11	06	327-330
Pooley, Julian	25	03	130-141	Roberts, Elizabeth	13	07	408-416
Porteous, J. Douglas	16	06	343-345		28	04	i-xvi
	17	07	391-395	Roberts, Gerrylynn K.	28	02	94-107
Porter, John	11	03	141-147	Roberts, Kenneth M.	03	01	39-42
Porter, R.E.	13	05	270-276	Roberts, Margery	01	08	252-255
Porter, Stephen	10	08	395-397		01	12	365-367
	12	01	36-37	Robins, F.W.	01	06	187-191
	23	04	199-204		01	09	278-282
Powell, Christopher	20	02	84-87		02	02	33-36
Powell, Michael	20	01	31-36		02	06	161-164
Preece, Patricia	20	02	73-79	Robinson, A.H.	04	01	35-36
	23	04	218-227		10	06	301-302
Priestley, E.J.	07	02	59-62	Robinson, E.J.	09	05	215-221
	10	03	139-141	Roche, T.W.E.	04	02	62-65
	16	05	284-287		04	03	95-97
Priestley, H.E.	04	03	110-115	Rodger, R.G.	14	02	98-100
Prince, Hugh C.	03	08	332-349	Roebuck, Peter	10	01	7-12
Pringle, Maura E.	17	03	135-140	Rogers, Alan	09	03	111-114
Pugh, Ralph B.	01	01	2-4		12	02	67-73
	13	01	15-22		19	01	21-26
Rackham, Oliver	27	02	66-77	Roper, Anne	01	01	9-12
Radmore, D.F.	09	05	222-225	Rowbotham, Herbert	04	05	185
Ramsey, A.R.J.	07	05	146-148	Rowley, Trevor	16	08	483-488
	07	06	192-195	Royle, Derek	28	03	176-180
	07	08	250-252	Royle, Stephen A.	14	02	79-90
	08	01	16-21		17	03	135-140
Ramskir, C.A.	10	05	227-233		18	03	136-141
Raymond, Stuart	12	03-04	156-157	Rubinstein, William D.	11	02	68-71
Read, Donald	06	04	121-124	Rudé, George	04	06	235-241
Redfern, John B.	15	05	259-271	Rugg, Julie	28	03	130-144
Redmonds, George	10	01	3-7	Rushton, Peter	13	08	481-487
	10	04	171-177	Ryan, Thomas	10	06	302-304
Redwood, B.C.	03	07	283-285	Rybotycki, Wieslaw	05	02	51-55
Reece, Susanna H.	28	02	94-107	Sanderson, Margaret	11	03	123-129
Reid, R.H.	04	07	282-290	Sasieni, L.S.	02	11	330-333
Resker, F.J.R.	02	08	251	Sayer, Michael	14	08	482-488
Reynolds, J.D	01	04	106-111	Scatchard, W.J.	10	07	332-333
	01	07	209-212	Schulenburg,			
	02	03	72-75	Alexander H.	28	02	109-122
Richards, Peter S.	08	01	10-15	Schurer, Kevin	16	06	335-342
	09	04	190-195		21	03	99-108
	12	05	241-245	Scotland, Nigel	13	05	259-262
	20	01	20-23	Seaborne, M.V.J.	05	05	151-154

INDEX OF AUTHORS

author	vol	no	pages	author	vol	no	pages
Seaman, Allan	16	05	278-281		02	06	172-175
Searby, Peter	25	03	153-163	Steel, David	12	02	93-101
Seliga, Joseph	28	04	225-241	Stenton, Doris M.	06	05	157-162
Serjeant, William	22	02	74-83	Stern, Elizabeth	13	06	346-348
	26	02	115-116	Stewart, Fran	13	03	149-159
Sharman, Frank A.	14	06	352-358	Stinchcombe, Owen	20	04	155-157
Sharp, Rita M.	21	04	156-161	Stones, Patricia R.	11	04	225-228
	24	03	153-163	Storey, Richard	12	08	394-400
Sharpe, Pamela	24	03	139-144	Stuart, Denis	21	01	16-19
Shaw, Gareth	13	04	205-209	Summers, P.G.	05	05	145-150
	29	03	167-182	Sunderland, N.	02	05	149-150
Sheail, John	09	02	59-64	Sutcliffe, Anthony	09	08	400-406
Sheeran, George	29	04	256-262		11	05	278-284
Sheeran, Yanina	29	04	256-262		16	02	67-72
Sheppard, June	18	03	106-111	Sutherland, Gillian	10	03	124-126
Sherry, D.	10	03	126-134	Swain, M. Burnham	05	03	85-89
Sherwood, Leslie	02	12	374-376	Swann, Brenda	07	07	232-240
Shirley, Bob	11	08	441-444	Swift, Roger	16	05	289-297
Shoda, K.	06	03	79-86	Tann, Jennifer	09	04	183-189
Short, Basil	15	06	358-360	Tapper, Oscar	06	01	22-24
Sill, Michael	12	02	74-79	Tate, W.E	01	02	38-42
	16	07	418-424		06	04	110-114
	17	04	205-211		06	05	171-174
Simpson, Elizabeth	14	05	259-261		08	04	126-130
Sitzia, Lorraine	27	04	218-224	Taylor, Antony	27	01	30-47
Skinner, Basil	09	07	353-356	Taylor, Christopher	14	04	195-201
Skipp, Victor	06	06	182-185	Teversham, T.F.	04	07	292-295
	14	06	325-331	Thacker, Helen	01	09	265-268
	14	07	392-399	Thirsk, Joan	04	04	129-133
Smart, Jim	29	03	152-166		04	05	182-184
Smith, Alan	11	02	72-76		06	05	166-169
Smith, Ann	25	04	231-241	Thomas, E.G.	14	07	400-406
Smith, Brian S.	08	03	106-108	Thomas, J.H.	08	02	42-46
Smith, Christopher J.	02	05	138-140	Thomas, James	15	04	212-217
	02	08	235-238	Thomas, Sylvia	19	04	170-173
	03	05	217-219	Thompson, Dorothy	03	01	13-19
	04	02	78-80	Thompson, James	07	04	126-132
Smith, David	19	01	16-17	Thompson, Kathryn	19	02	51-55
Smith, Janet	08	04	131-134	Thorburn, Dave	19	03	107-113
Smith, Jenny	24	02	91-101	Thornes, Vernon	24	01	37-43
Smith, Morris	09	08	379-386	Thornhill, Robert	02	12	372-373
Smith, Roger	09	01	27-35	Thorp, Jennifer	16	06	327-334
Spavold, Janet	26	02	89-101	Tibbott, S. Minwel	18	04	168-173
Spencer, K.M.	11	03	155-161	Tiller, Kate	14	03	131-133
Spittal, Jeffrey	19	04	147-158		17	02	107-108
Spufford, Margaret	10	08	398-400	Tillott, Peter M.	07	05	138-145
Spufford, Peter	05	06	173-176		08	01	2-10
	07	06	178-181	Timmins, Geoffrey	13	06	349-352
	09	07	357-361		15	01	6-20
Squires, Mike	27	03	163-182	Tinniswood, Adrian	15	04	195-203
Stanley-Morgan, Robert	02	01	11-15	Titterton, John	20	01	3-8
	02	04	106-110		25	02	88-94

INDEX OF AUTHORS

author	vol	no	pages	author	vol	no	pages
Todd, Nigel	11	05	285-289	Whyte, Ian D.	15	08	456-463
Torr, V.J.	01	05	159-162		17	01	4-10
Tranter, Margery	18	04	162-167	Whyte, Kathleen A.	15	08	456-463
Trinder, Barrie	09	06	289-293		17	01	4-10
	10	03	116-124	Wicks, A.T.	04	01	29-33
Tuffs, J.Elsden	03	06	264-266	Wikinson, Barbara	16	01	21-24
Tupling, G.H.	01	07	198-201	Wilde, D.S.	11	03	129-133
	01	08	234-237		12	05	228-234
	01	09	269-272	Wilde. Peter	12	03-04	152-156
	01	10	301-304	Wilkinson, Alan	15	07	402-405
	01	11	335-339	Wilkinson, Barbara	16	01	21-23
	01	12	361-364	Williams, A.R.	08	07	243-250
Turner, Brian	12	03-04	167-168		09	02	75-79
Turner, C.M.	07	02	63-65		10	01	27-32
Turner, Christopher B.	11	08	449-451	Williams, Huw	14	04	202-210
Turner, M.E.	29	01	14-24	Williams, Jack	25	02	95-108
Turner, Michael	12	01	18-25	Williams, L.R	18	02	65-68
Turner, Peter D.	16	07	412-417	Williams, Margaret H.	23	02	85-91
Turtle, James	19	01	16-17	Williams, Moelwyn I.	09	01	16-22
Twinn, Kenneth	09	03	115-120	Williams, Ned	20	03	118-122
Unwin, Joan	24	01	28-36	Willis, Arthur J.	04	01	12-22
	25	04	194-208		05	01	2-6
Upton, Christopher A.	28	01	16-23	Willis, Peter	06	03	91-96
Vaughan, J.E.	05	06	183-188	Willsher, Betty	23	02	66-84
	08	03	98-106	Wilmot, Frances	29	02	102-113
Wade Martins, Susanna	12	08	407-421	Wilson, John	14	08	478-480
Waites, Bryan	05	08	242-246	Wilson, Kenneth	02	08	232-234
	15	02	70-72		02	12	362-365
Walker, Andrew	29	04	223-230		03	07	305-307
Walker, Penelope	29	03	130-151		04	04	134-139
Walker, Peter	06	08	266-269		04	06	242-244
Walker, Peter T.	28	04	242-244	Winchester, Angus J.L.	21	02	70-75
Walmsley, Jan	20	01	9-19		27	01	3-17
Walton, John K.	13	06	323-331	Windeatt, Michael	05	01	17-22
	23	04	205-216	Withers, Charles W.J.	17	01	19-29
	24	02	91-101		18	03	127-135
	24	04	194-205	Wood, Sydney	14	08	471-476
	26	02	80-88	Woods, D.C.	14	08	454-459
Walton, John R.	10	06	271-276	Woodward, Donald M.	08	08	293-299
	17	06	343-350		09	02	89-95
Ward, Gordon	03	03	102-104		09	07	323-333
Warry, John	18	01	13-15	Woollard, Matthew	29	01	43-51
Waters, Ivor	02	07	212-214	Workman, Roy	14	05	262-269
Watson, C.H.B.	06	05	169-170	Worskett, Roy	12	05	204-206
Weiner, Edmund	24	03	164-173	Wrigh, M.D.	26	03	155-167
Weir, Christopher	28	01	24-35	Wrigley, Chris	16	01	36-48
White, Andrew	21	02	60-65		16	02	83-89
	28	02	78-93	Wrigley, E.A.	06	05	146-150
Whitehead, John	01	02	38-42		06	06	198-203
Whitting, Philip D.	01	12	371-373	Wulcko, Laurance	09	01	3-8
	04	02	84-85	Wyatt, Grace	15	03	132-134
	06	01	2-7	Yarham, E.R.	06	06	188-191

author	vol	no	pages	author	vol	no	pages
York, Brian	15	03	137-143				
Young, Colin	20	04	158-165				
Young, Craig	24	01	4-14				
Young, David	22	02	84-88				
Young, Rosa	14	06	341-347				

INDEX OF REVIEWERS

Although the *Amateur Historian* and the *Local Historian* have always included reviews of recently-published works, there was no consistent editorial policy with regard to this aspect of the journal in the early volumes. Many of the reviews were in the form of very short notices (sometimes only a couple of sentences), without any substantial attempt to assess merits or deficiencies, while the books and other publications reviewed were frequently not directly connected with local history. From the point of view of this index, however, the most significant limitation was that until the beginning of volume 9 reviews were either unsigned and unattributed, or were merely initialled. In consequence, this index covers volumes 9 to 29 inclusive and lists all reviewers whose articles appeared in those volumes. As will be seen, in the first ten or so volumes which are indexed, many of the reviewers contributed more than one, and sometimes several, shorter articles in one issue. In such instances each article has been separately listed.

reviewer	vol	no	pages	reviewer	vol	no	pages
Abrams, Lynn	21	03	134-135	Barringer,			
Alban, John R.	14	01	45-46	Christopher	13	01	47-50
Alcock, Nat	12	01	47-48		18	04	197-198
Alvey, Norman G.	24	01	57-58		25	01	51-53
	26	03	183	Barry, Jonathan	22	03	160-161
Ambler, R.W.	12	01	48-51	Baugh, G.C.	18	03	145
	13	03	172-175	Beard, Roy	10	06	318-319
	13	08	498-500		10	08	421-422
	15	02	101-103	Beattie, Derek	25	01	54-55
	15	06	375-376	Beckett, J.V.	12	01	53-54
	16	04	237-239		13	03	175-180
	16	05	315-316		14	05	300-301
	18	01	30-31		14	05	303-304
	19	02	77-79		14	07	436
	19	04	177-178		14	08	493-494
	19	04	180-181		14	08	498-499
	20	03	139-140		21	01	27
	22	02	103		22	03	161-162
	22	02	106-107	Beckett, John	13	04	237-238
Andrews, Jonathan	23	03	178-180	Beckwith, Ian	11	08	479-482
Archer, John	13	01	43-45	Beer, Albert	24	03	186-187
Ashman, Gordon	18	02	84-85	Beier, Lucinda			
Astill, G.C.	11	08	484-486	McCray	19	02	84
Aston, Michael	16	03	172-174	Bendall, Sarah	17	06	370-373
Auchterlonie, Mitzie	26	01	54-56		26	02	122-123
Baggs, Tony	09	03	148-149		29	03	184-185
Baker, T.F.T.	20	04	192-193	Bennison, Brian	27	02	119-120
	23	03	176-177	Beresford, Maurice	09	03	146-147
Barber, Peter	23	03	172-173	Bernard, Stanley	25	02	122
Barker, Philip A.	12	06	304-305				
	14	03	172-173				

INDEX OF REVIEWERS

reviewer	vol	no	pages	reviewer	vol	no	pages
Berry, Elizabeth	10	01	46-47	Carver, M.O.H.	16	07	432-433
Bettey, J.H.	09	05	248		16	07	433
	09	06	312-314		16	08	493
	10	01	45-46		16	08	493-494
	10	04	200-201	Challinor, P.J.	16	06	366-367
	11	08	477-479	Chaplin, Robin	09	04	202-204
	12	02	106-108		09	06	304-306
	12	08	439-440		09	08	409-410
	13	01	41-43		09	08	416
	13	04	235-237		10	01	46
	13	08	488-490		10	02	101-102
	13	08	497-498		10	03	154-156
	14	04	239-241		10	04	203-205
	15	01	49-50		10	06	306
	15	03	187-188		10	06	317-318
	15	03	188-189		11	06	350-354
	17	02	115-116		15	01	51-52
	19	01	32-34	Chapman, Colin R.	26	02	118-119
	21	03	136-137	Chapman, John	23	02	122
	21	04	179-180		24	01	56-57
	29	04	263-264		24	03	180-181
Black, Jeremy	22	03	158-159		27	01	53-54
	23	01	53-54	Chapman, Stanley D.	09	02	96-98
	24	01	54-56		12	02	104-106
	24	03	185-186	Charlton, Christopher	09	07	368-370
	26	01	52-53	Christie, Peter	22	04	215
	27	01	54-55		23	04	231-232
	29	04	266-267		24	04	250-251
Blackden, Stephanie	15	05	301-303		25	04	249-250
Blake, Robert	13	08	493-494		27	02	121
Blatchly, John	28	03	181		28	01	54-55
Bonney, Margaret	24	02	115-116		29	04	266
Bonsall, Mary	20	02	91-93	Church, Roy	10	03	152-153
Booker, John	10	02	102-103	Clark, Gillian	28	03	185-186
	10	03	151-152	Clarke, H.B.	10	06	312-313
	10	06	307-308	Clarke, Howard	11	08	482-484
Booth, D.T.N.	10	08	417-421	Collins, E.J.T.	17	03	182-184
Borsay, Peter	21	04	180-181	Corfield, P.J.	14	03	175-176
Bowles, Jackie	25	02	118-119	Coward, Barry	20	01	44-45
Bradbeer, John	22	04	219-220	Cox, Janice	19	01	31-32
Brigden, Roy	17	07	431-432	Cox, Jeff	16	08	499
	18	03	148	Cox, Nancy	16	06	365-366
	22	03	159-160	Cox, Ron	24	01	58-59
Brown, Sophie	28	04	247-249	Crosby, Alan G.	18	04	192-193
Burchall, Michael J.	15	02	97-99		19	03	130-132
Burge, Alan	13	04	244-245		20	03	140
Busby, Richard J.	09	01	36-38		21	01	33-34
Bushaway, R.W.	15	04	236-238		22	01	48
	15	05	297-300		24	02	118-119
	15	08	501-503		26	01	53-54
Butler, David M.	21	03	137		27	04	245-246
Campbell, Alan	23	01	52-53	Daniel, Robert	23	01	54-55

author	vol	no	pages	author	vol	no	pages
Dare, Edwin H.	27	02	123-124	Gaydon, Alec	09	02	95-96
David, Rob	19	01	36	Gelling, Margaret	12	06	307-308
	22	04	220-221		13	02	104-105
	23	03	180-181		13	06	366-367
David, Wayne	14	04	247-248		15	02	107-108
Deacon, Bernard	25	02	116		15	02	108
	26	02	120	Gelling, Peter S.	14	02	106-107
Dean, E. Barbara	17	02	121-122	Gerhardt, Paul	12	03-04	183-184
Dennier, Anne	20	04	197-198	Gerhold, Dorian	16	06	360-362
Dobson, R.B.	24	04	244-245	Gibson, Jeremy S.W.	13	01	45-47
Dore, Roy N.	14	08	502-504		24	04	246-248
Down, Kevin	12	05	252		28	04	245
	12	05	253-255	Glaisyer, E.B.	14	05	305-306
Doyle, Barry	21	04	181-193		14	05	306
Drake, Michael	27	02	119	Gooder, Arthur	10	08	425-426
Druker, Janet	13	05	303-306		11	02	95-96
Durie, Alistair J.	23	04	236-237	Gooder, Eileen	10	03	147-148
Dyer, Christopher	10	06	313-314		10	03	148-149
	10	08	424	Gourvishi, Terry	21	02	83-85
	14	03	171-172	Grant, Alison	23	02	119-120
	15	02	99-100	Grant, Alison	24	03	184-185
	15	04	232	Grant, Alison	28	01	56-57
	15	04	232-233	Gribble, M.G.	09	05	251-252
	15	04	233	Griffiths, Matthew	14	08	500-502
Dykes, D.W.	10	04	208-209		15	02	111-112
Dymond, David	25	04	246-247	Griffiths, Tom	24	03	181-182
	28	02	124	Grosvenor, Ian D.	14	05	293-294
Edwards, David	29	04	264		15	01	53-54
Egan, David	12	06	308-311		16	02	110-111
Ellis, Stanley	12	05	246-247	Hargreaves, John A.	14	02	110-111
Evans, David	14	04	241-244		14	07	432-433
	14	06	365-370		15	02	109-110
	14	08	494-496		23	02	116-117
	15	04	240-242		24	03	182-184
Evans, George Ewart	09	05	246-248		25	04	250-251
	09	07	364-365		26	03	179-180
	09	08	414-415		23	04	232-234
	10	03	153-154	Harley, J.B.	09	04	199-200
Evans, Neil	15	08	505-506		13	07	442-444
Evans, Nesta	16	07	436-437	Harris, Bryony	23	02	120
	22	03	162-163		26	01	57-58
	29	02	119-120	Harris, J.R.	15	05	303-305
Everitt, Alan	15	06	368-369		16	06	371-372
Everson, Paul	20	03	140-141		17	05	307-308
Field, Clive D.	29	01	58-60	Harris, Michael	20	01	43-44
Fletcher, Allan	27	01	57-58	Harrop, Sylvia	20	04	194-195
Fowkes, Dudley	18	04	200-201		21	02	79-80
Francis, Hywel	15	03	183-185	Hastings, Paul	26	01	56-57
Fraser, Constance M.	21	03	132	Haydon, Edwin	26	03	178
Fraser, I.A.	09	07	363-364	Hey, David	10	04	201-202
Garratt, Beverley	16	02	112		10	06	316-317
Garside, W.R.	19	03	132		17	02	123-125

INDEX OF REVIEWERS

reviewer	vol	no	pages	reviewer	vol	no	pages
Hey, David (cont.)	19	03	127	Jackson, Peter	26	02	117-118
	20	02	94-95	Jacobs, David	24	04	249-250
	20	03	141	James, Jude F.	11	05	298-299
	21	04	177-178	James, Tom Beaumont	27	01	52-53
	25	02	119-120	Jennings, Paul	27	03	186
	28	02	123-124	John, Trevor	14	04	237-239
Higgins, David	29	03	186-187		15	03	178-179
Hill, Robin	17	06	377	Jones, B.C.	21	01	29-31
	17	06	377-378	Jones, R. Merfyn	19	02	81-83
Hill, Sarah	16	06	358-359	Kamen, Henry	09	03	150-151
	17	06	375-377		09	08	417-418
	17	08	502-504	Kermode, Jenny	18	04	196-197
Hillaby, Joe	14	03	170-171	Kingsford, Peter	26	01	51-52
Hills, Catharine	13	08	500-501	Kuhlicke, F.W.	10	06	311-312
	15	02	107	Lane, Joan	09	02	101-102
Hilton, Rodney H.	09	04	198-199		09	08	411-412
	11	01	41-42	Lee, J.D.	09	08	410-411
	13	06	367-369	Leese, Roger	16	08	494-496
	15	02	108-109		18	02	86-87
Hodgetts, Michael	22	03	156-157	Levitt, John	19	01	34-35
Hodgson, Ralph	25	04	252-253	Lewis, Christopher P.	16	03	174-176
Holland, Derek	09	05	249-250		16	05	303-305
	09	08	418-419		17	01	55-57
	10	02	96-99		17	03	173-175
Hooke, Della	15	04	231-232		17	04	252
Hoose, Lucille	26	03	182		19	01	35-36
Horn, Pamela	22	03	157-158		21	04	178-179
Horrox, Rosemary	14	05	294-297	Lewis, Gwyn Iltyd	11	04	244
	14	05	304-305		11	05	296
	15	01	50-51		11	07	417-419
	15	02	100-101		12	06	303
	15	05	308-310		12	07	372-373
	29	02	114-115		13	02	105
Horton, Mark	17	03	175-177		13	02	116
	17	07	432-434		13	03	180
Hoskins, W.G.	09	07	362-363		13	03	245
	10	01	39-41		14	01	54
Hostettler, Eve	26	03	184-185		14	04	246
Houlbrooke, Ralph	28	03	182-183	Lifford, John	23	02	122-123
Howard-Drake, Jack	25	03	188		25	01	53-54
	29	01	56-57	Lloyd, David	17	05	299-300
Howells, Brian	13	06	375-376	Macleod, I.R.	17	03	184-186
	15	04	239-240	Malster, Robert	26	04	249-250
Howells, Jane	26	04	250-251	Marriott, John	20	01	46-47
Howkins, Alan	23	01	49-51	Marshall, J.D.	09	07	366-367
	27	02	121-123		14	01	48-50
Hull, Felix	26	04	246		14	03	182-183
	29	01	55-56		15	03	179-181
Hulton, Mary	14	03	173-175		22	02	104
Hutton, Barbara	12	03-04	169-171	Martin, John	29	02	115-116
Isserlin, Raphael M.J.	17	04	247-248	Mason, Hugh	25	04	245-246
Ives, E.W.	09	02	98-100	Maund, Kari L.	27	04	249-251

author	vol	no	pages	author	vol	no	pages
Maxted, Ian	23	04	234		11	07	421-424
	27	03	187		12	01	45-47
	29	03	185-186		12	01	55
McCord, Norman	10	07	361-366		12	01	56
	16	06	369-371		12	03-04	177-179
McLeod, Hugh	11	03	167-168		12	06	312-314
	15	02	112-113		12	07	373-376
Mercer, Eric	16	02	109-110		12	07	379-380
	17	02	114-115		13	02	108-115
Midwinter, Eric	09	03	152-153		13	04	238-242
Milburn, G.E.	20	04	195-196		13	06	369-374
Miles, Joyce C.	23	03	177-178		13	06	380
	24	03	181		13	07	444-445
Minchinton, Walter E.	11	04	242-243		14	02	107-110
	11	07	420-421		14	03	179-182
	11	08	488-491		14	04	246
Mitchell, P.	09	04	206-207		14	05	301-303
Mitchell, Sally-Anne	25	02	120-121		14	06	370-374
Morgan, Alun	12	05	248-251		14	08	496-497
Morgan, Philip	19	04	181		15	02	96-97
	19	04	182		15	05	305-307
	22	01	50-51		15	06	369-370
	22	04	213-214		15	07	438-439
	24	03	180		15	07	439-440
	27	02	118		15	08	506-507
Morgan, Victor	13	07	436-438		16	02	105-106
Morrill, John	28	01	55-56		18	02	82-83
Morton, Grenfell	17	08	499-501		29	02	114
Mullett, Michael	19	03	128-129	Mutch, Alistair	20	02	96
	20	02	93-94	Newall, Venetia	10	04	202
	22	02	101-103		12	07	367-368
	24	02	121-123		12	07	368-369
Mullins, Sam	18	01	28-29		13	07	438-439
Munby, D.	11	03	168-170	Newton, John	11	03	170-171
Munby, Lionel M.	02	11	347-350		11	06	359-361
	09	01	43		12	02	108-109
	09	01	47	Northeast, Peter	11	05	292-294
	09	01	47-48		11	06	354-356
	09	06	310-312		12	02	101-104
	09	08	418		12	07	369-372
	10	01	41-44		13	01	39-41
	10	01	44-45		13	06	374-375
	10	01	48		15	08	503-505
	10	03	150-151		23	04	230-231
	10	04	205-206		25	03	187-188
	10	04	209		27	04	247-248
	10	06	314-316	O'Carroll, Annette	28	01	59
	10	08	413-417	O'Day, Rosemary	10	07	367-368
	11	03	171-173		11	01	34-37
	11	06	356-357		11	01	40
	11	06	361		11	07	425-429
	11	07	414-417		12	01	51-53

reviewer	vol	no	pages	reviewer	vol	no	pages
O'Day, Rosemary *(cont.)*	12	03-04	173-177		23	04	237
	12	06	305-306		24	02	120-121
	13	02	116-117		26	03	180-181
	13	07	440-442	Rix, Michael	10	01	37-38
	14	06	363-365	Roake, Margaret	16	08	497-498
	15	04	235-236	Roberts,			
Oosthuizen, Susan	26	04	251-252	Elizabeth A.M.	16	05	305-307
Outhwaite, R.B.	09	03	145-146		17	07	429-431
	11	01	37-38		20	01	41-43
Owen, D.Huw	14	01	54-55		20	01	42-43
Owen, Trefor M.	16	06	367-368		21	03	135
	18	02	83-84		24	04	251-252
Palliser, D.M.	14	03	176-179	Robinson, David B.	09	07	365-366
	14	06	362-363	Roebuck, Peter	10	01	47
	15	02	103-106	Rogers, Alan	09	03	141-145
	16	04	236-237		09	06	308-310
Palmer, Marilyn	12	08	429-433		10	01	92-93
	13	01	52-53		11	05	294-295
Pam, David	14	08	492-493		12	03-04	171-172
Peberdy, Robert B.	16	05	309-311		12	03-04	172-173
	16	07	434-436		13	02	106
	17	04	248-252		13	06	377-379
	19	02	79-80		13	06	381
	21	01	31-32		14	01	53
	25	04	248-249		14	02	105-106
	27	03	183-185		14	02	117-118
Phillips, Vincent H.	13	02	106-108		14	04	245
Pilgrim, John E.	09	01	39-41		15	06	367
	09	02	100-101		15	06	367-368
Platt, Colin	20	04	190-191		23	02	116
Pooley, Colin G.	22	04	218-219		24	02	116-118
Porter, Stephen	25	01	55-56	Rollinson, William	09	03	149-150
Powell, John	16	06	364		09	04	207
Power, Michael J.	27	03	185-186		10	03	149-150
Powlesland, John	25	02	122-123		19	03	132-133
Prescott, Tim	28	03	187		21	03	131
Pringle, Roger	11	02	96-99	Rose, Julia	29	02	121-122
	15	06	371-374	Rose, Louise	23	01	56-58
Quinnell, Henrietta	23	02	115	Rose, Mary B.	19	02	83-84
	25	01	49	Rose, Michael E.	22	04	216-218
Ranger, Paul	21	04	183	Rowe, John	23	03	181
Rau, Diana	27	01	55-56		24	01	53-54
Ravensdale, Jack R.	11	06	357-359		29	02	120-121
Raymond, Stuart A.	26	04	247-248	Rowland-Jones, Mark	17	07	436-438
Razzell, Peter	28	03	183-185		17	04	253-255
Read, Gordon	19	04	178-180	Rowlands, Marie B.	14	05	308-309
Reed, Michael	28	04	249-250		14	05	309
Reid, Caroline	11	08	487-488		21	01	32-33
	12	08	433-435	Rowley, John	16	05	307-308
	14	01	46-48	Rowley, R.T.	18	01	31-33
Richards, Jeffrey	21	03	132-133	Rowley, Trevor	12	01	54-55
Riley, Ray	23	02	123		12	02	112-115

author	vol	no	pages	author	vol	no	pages
Rowley, Trevor *(cont.)*	14	02	112-115		18	03	146-148
Rumble, Alexander	19	02	81	Sutcliffe, Anthony	10	06	310-311
Russell, Rex C.	14	08	497-498		11	01	42-43
	15	01	52-53		11	07	419-420
Sanders, Peter	20	02	90-91		12	06	315-320
Scherr, Jennifer	19	03	129-130	Swailes, Paul	28	04	246-247
Schorb, Brenda D.	21	01	28-29	Swanzy, Kay T.	09	05	252-254
Searby, Peter	09	04	201-202		09	08	407-409
	09	04	204-206	Tann, Jennifer	09	01	44
Sharp, Barbara	21	01	34-35		09	01	45-46
Shearing, Edwin A.	13	05	300-303		09	03	151-152
Shooter, R.A.	25	04	251-252		09	04	200-201
Shotter, David	21	01	35-36	Taylor, Christopher C.	09	05	250-251
Simpson, Jacqueline	12	07	365-367		24	01	52-53
Skinner, Basil	09	07	367-368		25	01	51
	09	08	415	Thirsk, Joan	13	01	50-52
	10	04	210-211	Thompson, Kate	24	02	123-124
Slater, Terry R.	12	08	437-439		28	04	246
	13	02	103-104	Thornton, Christopher	20	02	95-96
	13	02	117-119				
	13	04	242-244	Thorpe, H.	10	08	422-424
	16	02	106-109	Tiller, Kate	16	04	244-247
Smith, A. Hassell	14	02	115-116		17	01	58-59
Smith, Graham R.	25	02	117-118		17	05	302-306
Smith, J.T.	10	01	35-37		21	02	80-81
Snell, Keith D.M.	23	02	118	Tillott, P.M.	09	01	41-43
	23	04	234-235		09	03	147-148
	24	02	119-120	Timmins, Geoff	21	02	83
	24	04	245-246	Trinder, Barrie	09	08	412-413
	26	02	121-122		10	02	89-91
	27	04	251-252		10	04	206-208
	28	01	53-54		10	06	309-310
	29	02	116-117		11	01	38-39
Spruce, Derek	28	03	186		11	04	238-242
Stamper, Paul	22	04	215-216		11	05	297-298
	23	04	230		12	02	111-112
Stapleton, Barry	28	02	125		12	03-04	179-181
Steppler, Glenn A.	17	08	501-502		12	03-04	181-182
	23	01	55-56		12	07	376-377
Stitt, F.B.	14	05	307-308		12	08	435-437
Stratton, Michael	16	03	176-177		13	03	169-170
	16	03	179-181		13	03	170-172
	16	05	313-315		13	05	299-300
	16	07	438-440		13	05	306-307
	17	02	122-123		13	08	494-496
	17	03	179-182		14	01	50-53
	17	06	378-379		14	07	434-435
	18	01	33-34		15	03	181
	18	03	146		15	03	185-187
Stuart, Denis	13	08	490-492		15	07	436-438
	27	04	246-247		16	02	104-105
Summers, Anne	17	07	427-429		16	03	181-183

reviewer	vol	no	pages	reviewer	vol	no	pages
Trinder, Barrie (cont.)	16	04	241-244	Whitting, Philip	10	02	88-89
	16	04	247		10	06	305
	16	04	248		12	02	115-116
	16	06	368-369	Whyman, John	12	07	377-379
	16	06	372-373		15	01	54-56
	16	08	498-499	Whyte, Ian	18	04	194-196
	16	08	500-503		20	04	193-194
	17	03	186	Wickes, Michael	23	01	58-59
	17	03	186-187		26	04	248
	17	05	306-307	Wild, G.	10	02	99-101
	17	05	308-309	Wilkins, J.W.J.	11	07	424-425
	17	05	309-310	Williams, Chris	28	04	250-251
	17	05	310	Williams, Huw	13	08	496-497
	17	05	310-311	Williams, Paul	23	03	173-175
	17	06	374-375		26	02	123-124
	17	07	434-435	Wilson, Alan	29	03	183-184
	17	07	435	Wilson, R.M.	10	07	366-367
	17	07	436	Winchester, Angus	16	04	239-241
	18	01	34-35		18	04	193-194
	18	01	35		18	04	198-200
	18	01	35-36		20	01	45-46
	18	02	85-86		20	01	47-48
	22	01	48-49		20	04	191-192
Trueman, Michael	17	07	434		21	02	82
Vaisey, David	17	01	51-55		21	02	85
	17	03	177-179		22	02	105-106
	17	07	426-427		23	01	59
Vass, Pamela	29	01	57-58	Winstanley, Michael	20	04	196-197
Wade Martins,				Winterbotham, Diana	22	02	99-100
Susanna	20	03	137-139	Wood, Oliver	14	08	499-500
Wakelin, Peter	16	03	177-179	Woodward, Donald	10	02	93-96
	16	05	311-313		10	07	368-369
	17	02	117-118		11	02	100-101
	17	05	301-302		12	02	109-110
Walton, John K.	17	02	118-121		12	02	110-111
	27	01	56-57		12	05	251-252
	28	01	57-58	Wormleighton, Tim	24	04	248-249
Wanklyn,				Wyke, Terry	23	03	175-176
Malcolm D.G.	16	06	362-363	Wykes, David L.	23	02	121-122
	17	08	497-499	Yarrow, Philip	29	04	267-268
	17	08	499	Yorke, Barbara	25	01	50
Wardman, John	26	01	50-51	Youings, Joyce	25	03	186
Webb, Katherine	29	04	265				
Webster, Graham	10	06	308-309				
	11	01	40-41				
	11	01	44-45				
Wells, Roger	21	01	28				
	23	01	51-52				
	27	04	248-249				
	29	02	117-119				
Whitehead, David	15	03	181-182				
	15	04	233-235				